PLEASE DON'T FEED THE LIONS

Michael A. Vander Klipp

CRC Publications
Grand Rapids, Michigan

Text illustrations: Tim Foley

Copyright © 1995, CRC Publications, 2850 Kalamazoo Avenue SE, Grand Rapids, Michigan, 49560.

All rights reserved. With the exception of brief excerpts for review purposes, no part of this book may be reproduced in any manner whatsoever without written permission from the publisher. Printed in the United States of America on recycled paper. ♻

ISBN 1-56212-062-X

Library of Congress Data
Vander Klipp, Michael A., 1964–
   Please don't feed the lions / Michael A. Vander Klipp.
      p. cm.
      1. Bible. O.T. Daniel—Meditations—Juvenile literature.
[1. Bible. O.T. Daniel—Meditations. 2. Prayer books and devotions. 3. Christian life.] I. Title.
BS1555.4.V36   1995
224'.509505—dc20   94-46166
                                                                      CIP
                                                                      AC

10 9 8 7 6 5 4 3 2 1

CONTENTS

Preface 5

Daniel and Friends in a New Land
Meditations 1-8. 8

Nebuchadnezzar's Disturbing Dream
Meditations 9-14. 26

A Skinny Statue and a Fiery Furnace
Meditations 15-22. 40

King Nebuchadnezzar Learns a Beastly Lesson
Meditations 23-26 58

Divine Graffiti
Meditations 27-30. 68

Daniel's Night with the Big Cats
Meditations 31-40. 78

PREFACE

The book of Daniel tells the tale of four innocent, back-country boys dumped unwillingly into the power center of a corrupt empire. These stories make wonderful reading. They are well-written and entertaining, and they do an excellent job of presenting the striking contrast between the values and life priorities of the exiled Jews and those of the people of Babylon. But even more important, the Daniel stories picture a God who is Lord of every nation on earth and who is able to protect and guide his people no matter where they may find themselves in this wide world. God is the hero of the book of Daniel.

The forty meditations in this little book will help you view Daniel and his three friends with sympathetic eyes, understand better the situation and choices they faced, and appreciate their solid faith in God. They will also speak to the similar, if less dramatic, situations you may face each day and challenge you to trust God as Daniel, Shadrach, Meshach, and Abednego did.

Michael A. Vander Klipp, author of *Please Don't Feed the Lions*, is an associate editor for Zondervan Publishing House.

Harvey A. Smit
Editor in Chief
Education Department

DANIEL AND FRIENDS IN A NEW LAND

When we first meet Daniel and his friends Hananiah, Mishael, and Azariah, they've just been chosen to train for work in King Nebuchadnezzar's court. These young Hebrews, recently captured from the land of Judah and taken to Babylon, are the best and brightest of the Jewish people.

Meditation 1

WHERE ARE YOU, GOD?

READ DANIEL 1:1-2

Rick rubbed his chin and winced in pain. He was nearly alone in the school hallway—just him and the janitor. The old man looked at Rick like he was some kind of circus freak, then quickly turned away and went back to sweeping up loose bits of dust and paper with his red rag mop.

"What am I going to do?" Rick thought as he slumped to the floor and looked at his scuffed-up high-tops. That's when he noticed the hole in his jeans. "Way to go, Ace. Mom's going to *love* that," he mumbled to himself. Here he was, all alone in a big, strange school. He had checked all the parking lots for the bus from his school, but couldn't find it anywhere. He was convinced that his class had left without him. What was worse, he didn't even have a quarter in his pocket to call home.

What a horrible day this had been! And it had all started out so well. His class had traveled across town to the big middle school for a group rally with other fifth- and sixth-grade classes from around the city. They had come to hear a professional basketball player talk to them about staying away from drugs and doing their best in school.

Rick had really wanted to get the player's autograph. So as soon as the rally was over, he bolted down the steep steps of the bleachers. About halfway down he accidentally bumped into a rough-looking kid—a guy about his age, but twice as big.

"Hey, watch where you're going, twerp!" the miniature version of King Kong snarled, grabbing Rick's shirt. In seconds, the 140-pound punching machine with a brush cut was all over Rick. He took two quick cuffs to the eye and chin before he sprawled backwards into a group of squealing girls.

Kong Jr. had wanted more, but a massive phys ed teacher grabbed him by the back of his black leather jacket. As the teacher pulled him down the bleachers, the tough guy had yelled, "You punk! Nobody gets me in trouble and gets away with it—I'll get you for this!"

As soon as the room stopped spinning, Rick had tried to collect himself. When the fog in his head cleared, he had looked out on the platform to see his hoops hero mobbed by kids. "Well, if I can't get *his* autograph," Rick had muttered, "at least I have the knuckle prints of a future professional wrestling champ on my face. That kid could have knocked out Hulk Hogan."

Back in the hallway, the janitor turned out the lights. As Rick sat alone in the darkness, he complained, "Guess being a Christian doesn't count. Where was God when I needed him?"

That must be what the people of Judah were thinking as we read about them in today's passage. The writer of the book of Daniel talks about the king of Babylon and says that "The Lord delivered Jehoikim King of Judah into his hand." Why? Because the people had sinned— they hadn't lived according to God's commands.

Dazed, confused, hurting from losing their fight, God's people must have wondered what had happened to them. How did they get to this strange place? Where was God when the going got tough? They hadn't recognized the extent of their sin. They didn't know that God was sending them into exile in Babylon so that their hearts would turn, once again, to him. Even though they had sinned, these were still God's chosen people. And God never intended to leave his people alone in this strange land.

In this book of devotions we'll be looking at God's love and watchful care for people. We'll see how God stays faithful to those who love him, no matter what the situation. And we'll see how God showed his power to the people of Babylon.

"Hey Rick!" Rick's heart jumped at the sound of his best friend's voice. "Where have you been, buddy? We've been waiting for you for twenty-five minutes!" Rick stood up and looked past his friend. He saw the big yellow bus filled with his classmates. In his confusion, he had never thought to look in the most obvious place—the front driveway!

> Lord, sometimes I feel lost and afraid.
> Sometimes it seems like you're very far away.
> Thank you that I can always trust in your
> watchful care over me, no matter what.
> Amen.

Meditation 2

NEW LAND, SAME GOD

READ DANIEL 1:3-5

Juan sat down at his desk and took a quiz paper from the girl who passed them down the aisle. As he looked down at the page, he started to sweat. Many of the words made no sense to him! Suddenly, Juan didn't feel so good. His head spun and his stomach churned. He rested his damp forehead in his hand and closed his eyes.

"Why did I have to come to this place?" Juan asked himself quietly. "I want to go back home . . . back to all my friends. Back to my own school."

Juan thought back to his home in El Salvador. How wonderful it had been when his family was all together in that house! But that was before the police came and took his father away. Although his father had committed no crime, the government had thrown him in jail. Juan's mother had been trying ever since to get him released.

After their father's imprisonment, Juan and his little sister Teresa had traveled to Canada to live with their aunt. Their mother had sent them there so they would be safe from the fighting. She had promised that as soon as their father was released, they would all be together again. They would start a new life in Canada.

Juan couldn't wait for that day. But meanwhile he had this quiz. What was he going to do?

Perhaps Daniel and his friends could give Juan some advice. You see, they were in a similar situation. Soldiers had forced them from their homes and dragged them from their land. They had been forced to work for Nebuchadnezzar, the king of this place called Babylon. To do that, they first had to learn a strange new language. Then they had to become straight-A students.

Their task was not an easy one. All their lives they had been taught that there was only one God. They believed in that God with all their hearts. Now they were in Babylon, a place where people believed in hundreds of gods. They were to be educated in Babylon's toughest school. And they were to eat from the king's table. Just imagine how strange Daniel and his friends must have felt!

You might wonder why the king chose these slaves for his service instead of telling his servant Ashpenaz to select men from Babylon's richest families. After all, many young Babylonian men probably would have jumped at the chance to enter the king's service. Why were these Hebrews being educated instead of the best young men of Babylon?

Actually, many of the kings of that time did just what Nebuchadnezzar did—and with good reason. If Nebuchadnezzar selected from among the rich young men of Babylon, their families would ask for special perks and favors. And such young men would probably be more concerned about their family's social standing than about loyalty to the king. But Daniel, Hananiah, Mishael, and Azariah were prisoners in this new land. They had nothing, and Nebuchadnezzar was offering them everything—education, rich food and clothing, and all kinds of special treatment. By doing so, the king hoped to earn their complete loyalty.

Little did he know that the God of the Hebrews, the one true God, also demanded their loyalty. And these four young Hebrews, as we shall see throughout this book, were determined to remain faithful to their God.

Ashpenaz chose these young men for their brains and their looks. God chose them because he knew their hearts.

God knows Juan's heart too. He knows that Juan and his family love him. And God will be with this family in Canada just as he was with four young Hebrews in Babylon so many years ago.

*Dear God, sometimes bad things happen. Sometimes we feel like our lives will never get better. Help us to know that you have a plan for us, no matter what happens. Help us to be patient enough to see where you will lead us.
Amen.*

Meditation 3

WHAT'S IN A NAME?

READ DANIEL 1:6-7

8:04. 8:05. 8:06. Where was Miss Jules?

8:07. Still no sign of their teacher. Many of the kids in the class chattered excitedly to each other. What if Principal MacReedy didn't know that Miss Jules wasn't in class? What if nobody came into their class all day? If they kept quiet enough, they could talk and play and mess around all day without anyone knowing.

8:12. 8:13. Some of the kids started shooting paper wads into the wastebasket and imitating sports announcers: "He shoots from the backcourt . . . and he SCORES!" Others kids sat on their friends' desks, talking and laughing.

At 8:14 the door swung wide open. "Awwww!" everyone in the class moaned. A strange-looking man stepped into the room, followed by Principal MacReedy. "Calm down, class, and get back to your seats," the principal said. "What is this, the NBA playoffs or something? You boys pick up all this paper and sit down."

"Miss Jules is not feeling well today. She has a nasty case of the flu, and she could be out for a few days. So this gentleman here will be your substitute teacher until Miss Jules gets well. His name is Mr. Beetle. I expect you to show him the same kind of respect that you show Miss Jules." The principal turned on his heel and walked out the door.

"Hello, kiddies!" Mr. Beetle smiled. "How are you all doing? I bet we're going to have lots of fun together." When he took off his snow-covered coat and hat, his frizzy red hair sprang out in all directions. He wore a dark green sweater and a bright yellow tie. His brown pants were rumpled and baggy.

"Looks like a pushover," Jason whispered to his best buddy Mike. "Yeah. It's party time!" Mike whispered back, smirking at the rest of the class.

"Let me tell you a little about myself," Mr. Beetle said. "First of all, I have thirty cats at home. Second, I'm terrible with names, because I substitute teach all the time. So here's how we'll do it. Since there are thirty kids in this class, I'm going to call each one of you by one of my cat's names. You there in the blue shirt—you remind me of Daisy. And you with the red hair—you look like my cat Tomato."

On and on Mr. Beetle went until he had named all thirty kids after each of his cats. Jason and Mike were now Pepper and Scats. Gina and Lisa were Lulabelle and Muffy. They were all so stunned by their new teacher's behavior that they forgot about their plans to party.

How would you like to get a new name? Even worse—How would you like to be named after somebody's *cat*? The kids in Miss Jules's class probably felt a lot like Daniel and his three friends in today's passage.

The names Daniel, Hananiah, Mishael, and Azariah meant something in Hebrew culture. *Daniel* meant "God is my Judge"; *Hananiah* meant "The LORD shows grace"; *Mishael* meant "Who is what God is?"; *Azariah* meant "The LORD helps." Their parents gave them these names to remind them of who they were and who their God was.

The new names that Ashpenaz gave them—Belteshazzar, Shadrach, Meshach, and Abednego—all referred to names of Babylonian gods. It was as insulting for these four young men to be named after false gods as it was for Gina, Lisa, Jason, and Mike to be named after a passel of flea-bitten mice-chasers.

Still, God knew them. Just because they had to take on new names didn't mean that they would lose their love for the God of Israel. God was more powerful than the false gods of Babylon—and these four young men knew it. They were determined to remain faithful to their Lord.

By the way, Pepper and Scats were sent to Principal MacReedy's office. Seems Mr. Beetle wasn't too pleased when they asked if they could both go to the litter box.

> Lord, you know who I am and how I feel about you. I thank you that, no matter what happens to me, I can come to you in prayer. Thank you for answering me and for knowing me by name.
> Amen.

Meditation 4

DANIEL'S STRANGE MENU (PART 1)

READ DANIEL 1:5, 8-14

In this passage we see Daniel and his friends sitting around the king's table. These young men didn't get a break from their schooling at mealtime—the dinner table was just a different classroom for them. They had to learn about all the aspects of the king's culture if they were going to work for him.

So the king's servants passed huge, steaming plates full of delicious food in front of these young Hebrews. Slabs of hot meat and gravy. Thick, crusty breads smothered in butter. Deep red wine to drink. Just thinking about it was enough to make a person's mouth water!

Daniel took one whiff of the food. "No, thanks," he said to Ashpenaz, the king's chief official. "My pals and I will just nibble off the salad bar."

I suppose Daniel's mother would have been proud. So would his doctor. But people in those days never really worried about eating right or avoiding things like salt and fat. So why did Daniel and the others refuse all that wonderful food?

Well, for a couple of pretty good reasons. First of all, the Hebrew people had rules about which foods they could eat. The book of Leviticus, part of our Old Testament, includes many of those rules. Some foods were called "clean," which meant that they were O.K. for God's people to eat. Other foods were "unclean." For example, in Daniel's time you would never have caught a Jew chowing down on ham and bacon for breakfast. Pork was considered unclean.

Many years before Daniel was born, God gave his people these rules about what they could and couldn't eat. Since Daniel couldn't be certain that those steaming plates of meat were "clean," he decided not to chance it.

The second reason Daniel rejected the food had to do with his devotion to God. Back in Daniel's time, people didn't just pop a frozen dinner into the microwave on their way to the den to watch *Jeopardy*. Families and friends took mealtimes very seriously. Eating together was a major social event, and to sit and eat with someone meant you were friends.

Daniel didn't want people to think that he and his friends had given in to King Nebuchadnezzar. He didn't want the Hebrews to think that he had abandoned the true God. He didn't want to be considered a close personal friend of this Babylonian ruler. So he asked to be excused from the king's table.

Ashpenaz was a little nervous about Daniel's request. Would the king get mad at *him* when he saw Daniel and the others looking skinny and underfed? "Aaah, no. I don't think so," he said to Daniel.

Daniel was stuck, but he wouldn't give up. The Scripture reading for today tells us that Daniel cut a deal with the guard so that his plan would work. Imagine that guard standing by the table, watching these young men eat all that delicious food. I'm sure his stomach was growling—and I'm sure Daniel knew it! So the next time the servant took food to the table, Daniel said to the guard, "Hey, pal, I see the king makes you live on veggies and water."

"Yeah, so what?" the guard growled.

"How would you like a change of menu?" Daniel offered. "How would you like to switch with me and eat from the king's table?"

The guard's jaw dropped. "You've got to be kidding. You mean to tell me you'd trade this delicious food for a bunch of dried-out carrots and celery? You've got a deal!"

Daniel probably grinned and told his friends that his plan was starting to work. They were all happy they would be able to do what was right.

*Dear God, sometimes it can be hard to do the things that you want us to do. Yet you help us know what is right. Even though others try to stop us, help us always to do what pleases you most.
Amen.*

Meditation 5

DANIEL'S STRANGE MENU (PART 2)

READ DANIEL 1:15-16

"I can't believe how lucky I am," the king's guard thought as he took another huge bite off the drumstick. "Those Hebrews sure are a strange bunch. Imagine trading this feast for vegetables and water!" He shook his head and sopped the gravy off his plate with a chunk of thick bread.

Any of us might think the same way. Can't you just see Daniel and his friends crunching and munching their way through every meal? Perhaps this could be considered history's first successful diet plan: "Daniel's Sure-fire Diet: guaranteed to keep you fit and trim. Also guaranteed to make God happy."

Look at the results of this experiment. When the time came for Daniel, Shadrach, Meshach, and Abednego to stand up next to the other young men, they were judged "healthier and better nourished" than the rest. The guard was pleased with the results, and the four young Hebrews were allowed to continue with their special menu.

So what's the lesson for us in this passage? The next time we order a big, juicy burger, should we say "hold the beef" instead of saying "hold the onions"? Instead of having Thanksgiving turkey, should we carve into a big Thanksgiving turnip? And the next time we go to the baseball park and order a hot dog, should we switch the sausage on the bun for a carrot with mustard?

True, rich, fatty foods aren't always the best for us. But God isn't using this passage to give us tips for the healthiest salad selections either. Let's look a little deeper.

In our last meditation, we learned that Daniel wanted to avoid the king's food for some very good reasons. The main idea behind the veggies-and-water diet plan was to keep Daniel and his friends "clean" and loyal to God. These four men had faith that God would see them through this test. Daniel and his friends knew that God would bless them for their loyalty.

God was pleased with this small act and blessed them, as we shall see, with more than just good physical health. He also gave them brain power and wisdom. These four men became very popular with the government officials. They were on the fast track to the top of the Babylonian government . . . at least for the moment.

This two-part look at Daniel's act of loyalty to God will help us as we continue through the book of Daniel. These four men would face far more difficult tests in the months and years to come. God knew that if Daniel could stand up to Ashpenaz now, he would be able to stand up to King Nebuchadnezzar later. If Daniel was courageous enough to demand carrots now, he would also be courageous enough to face lions when the time came.

Standing up for God can be difficult at times. Sometimes we don't want to get up from the table and head to the salad bar. Passing up something that looks fun, even though we know it's wrong, is tough. And standing up for God can be especially hard if we have to stand up to our own friends.

It probably would have been easy for Daniel and the others just to eat the king's food, just as it's often easy for us to go along with the crowd. But God is pleased when we take a stand for him. And when we prove that we can be trusted with small problems, God gives us wisdom to deal with the big problems that come our way later on.

> Dear God, I want to serve you today. I want you to know you can trust me to take a stand for you, even when doing wrong would be so easy. Thank you for giving me strength to follow you.
> Amen.

Meditation 6

LOOK FOR YOUR GIFTS!

READ DANIEL 1:17

Jennifer woke up early on her birthday, even though it was summer. She had been out of school for two weeks and had been looking forward to this day for a long time.

Her father had told her two days ago that he had bought her just what she wanted this year. She was sure she was going to get a new soccer ball and cleats for her summer soccer league. For the past two years she had played without cleats. Now that she was getting better at the game, she needed those new shoes. Sometimes the field was muddy or damp, and she had to be careful not to fall. New cleats would boost her game up a notch—she was sure of it!

When she ran downstairs, she saw a note from her dad. "Jennifer," the note read, "if you want to find your present, look for it where the dog catches rays."

The den! That's where Buffy loved to lie in the sun. She ran through the kitchen to the small room. Sure enough—there was her present, all wrapped up, tied with a bow, and sitting on the desk. But it sure was an odd-looking box. How did her dad fit a pair of cleats in there? And where was the soccer ball? Maybe there would be another note.

As she tore into the present, her dad stepped into the doorway with a big smile. "Happy birthday, sweetheart!" he said.

Jennifer tried to look happy. Actually, she did a good job of acting really excited. She hugged her dad and smiled after she took her brand-new flute out of its case.

Although she had been in band for two years, Jennifer had never told her father that she just couldn't get the hang of reading music. Whenever the band played in assembly, Jennifer would pretty much fake it. But this flute was an expensive present—something she knew her dad had to save up to buy. So she decided to hide her disappointment.

In today's passage, we read about the gifts God gave to Daniel, Shadrach, Meshach, and Abednego. God gave them "knowledge and understanding of all kinds of literature and learning." In other words, they could knock the socks off of any written test their Babylonian teachers could dish out. And to Daniel, God gave a special gift—the ability to explain dreams.

As we will learn, these four young men didn't hide their gifts; they put them to work. Daniel and his friends knew that God had blessed them, and they weren't afraid to use and increase their abilities in order to please God.

Jennifer knew what her talents were, too, and playing the flute was not one of them! So she decided to tell her dad about her feelings. She admitted to him that she thought the soccer ball and cleats would help her out more than the flute.

But her father wanted her to at least give the flute a try. Without her knowing, good old Dad had volunteered Jennifer for a flute solo at church. She was to play while the offering was being collected.

Jennifer decided to do her best to make her father proud. When it was time for her to play, she stood in front of the small congregation and played her heart out.

Dad took her to the sporting goods store as soon as it opened on Monday morning!

Dear God, thank you for giving me talents and abilities. I know that you want me to do the best I can with my gifts. Help me to look hard for my gifts and then to use them for you.
Amen.

Meditation 7

RAISE THAT HAND!

READ DANIEL 1:18

"And now, class, can anyone tell me what the capital of Guatemala is?"

Hector knew the answer to that question. "Obviously," he thought to himself, "it's Guatemala City. Anybody knows that. Why can't Mr. Runder ask harder questions?" But Hector didn't say anything.

Mr. Runder's frustration showed. "All right people, what's the deal? This is all material we have studied before. Now come on. Who can tell me the answer?"

"What a bunch of dimwits," Hector thought, smirking to himself. He felt proud that he knew so much about Central America. He had studied the map of Guatemala in the textbook. He had even been there once to visit his uncle. But still, Hector said nothing.

Have you ever acted this way in class? Perhaps you didn't raise your hand because you weren't sure of the answer. (I did that all the time in my math classes.) Or maybe you didn't want to answer because you thought that then the teacher would ask you another, even harder question. Or maybe you were like Hector and didn't raise your hand because you just didn't *feel* like it.

What would Daniel have done in Hector's position?

Well, let's see what today's passage says about our four friends. They had reached their biggest test. They had to stand before King Nebuchadnezzar and be reviewed.

Ashpenaz's work was done. He had done his best to educate these men in Babylonian culture, and they had done well. Ashpenaz was proud—he knew that he had done a good job.

God knew it too. As these young men stood in the presence of this earthly king, God, the heavenly King, was pleased. Not only had they passed Ashpenaz's tests, but they had also passed God's test. These men had learned about all of Babylon's strange gods, but they hadn't given up their love for the one true God. Yes, they had passed the most important test of all.

Have you passed God's test? Are you ready to be used by him to work in his kingdom? There are any number of ways that you can pass God's test. All you have to do is raise your hand and be ready to be called on.

Maybe God wants you to serve him by being a friend to the new kid in class. Or maybe God would like you to do some yard work for your older neighbor. God might even be testing you to see if you will keep your promise to feed and walk the dog every day. Look around and try to find small ways to serve God in your everyday life. And when God tests you, be ready to raise your hand and answer God's call.

Maybe Hector should have taken this advice. When his parents got home from parent/teacher conferences, they grilled him about his low marks in class participation. Hector sure answered questions that night!

*Dear God, thank you for giving me many chances to serve you. I pray that you will help me as I look for ways to do what you want me to do. Then, when I find a way to serve you, give me the courage to raise my hand and be called on for you.
Amen.*

Meditation 8

COACH'S PET

READ DANIEL 1:19-21

KABLAAAM!

Big Murray slammed the ball hard with his big wooden bat. "Woah! He sure got all of that one," Jeremy said to himself as he watched the ball fly straight out to him.

It was a high pop fly out to left field. The ball soared up into sky—for a minute it looked like it would go into orbit. But Jeremy thought it would be an easy catch, so he didn't move toward the ball like his little league coach had told him to do a hundred times in practice.

Just then a gust of wind caught the ball, shifting it toward center field. Panicked, Jeremy scrambled as fast as he could to catch the ball. "I'll never reach it!" he yelled, stumbling over the wet turf.

Suddenly Jeremy saw a flash of white out of the corner of his eye. Tisha sprinted past him and dove head-first for the baseball. Just as she stretched out to grab the ball, she hit the deck—hard.

How she held on to that baseball, Jeremy would never know. He watched as Tisha stood up and tried to wipe the mud off her white uniform. She was smeared with the sticky brown goo from head to toe. "Nice grab, Tisha," Jeremy said weakly as she trotted past him toward her position at second base.

Jeremy headed back to left field and scowled. "Coach's pet," he grumbled to himself. "I can't believe she would steal that out from me. I almost had it too." Jeremy worked hard at thinking up new reasons to be mad at Tisha. "What a show-off. Why would she dive for the ball? It's not like the game was on the line or anything. This is only the third inning!" The more Jeremy thought, the madder he got.

Jeremy reminds me of the "magicians and enchanters" that we read about in today's passage. These men, members of the king's court, advised on important decisions. They were his trusted wise men. A few of them must have been in the room as King Nebuchadnezzar tested Daniel and his friends.

How they must have grumbled at the success of these four young men! Who were these foreigners who thought they could take the place of these wise men? And how did they get to know so much about the wisdom of Babylon?

"Ashpenaz, my good servant," Nebuchadnezzar must have said, "you have done very well with these young men. Why, I'd say these youngsters are *ten times* smarter than any of my magicians or enchanters!"

Can't you just *see* the smoke pouring out of the wise men's ears? "King's pet," they probably complained. "I could have answered that question too (if I had studied that subject). Old Nebuchadnezzar is just being soft on these guys because they're from a faraway country." Still, I bet those advisors were more than a little were worried about their job security.

Tisha is like Daniel, Shadrach, Meshach, and Abednego. She practiced hard and followed her coach's instructions. She came out to the ball field ready to play. The four young men were also prepared to face the king. They had studied hard so that, no matter what Nebuchadnezzar asked, they would be prepared. They knew that God would see them through.

How hard do you work at doing your best? Do you work hard at digging up excuses? Let me tell you, excuses don't get you anywhere.

Just ask Jeremy. After his lazy display in the third inning and his sour attitude in the fourth and fifth innings, Coach took him out of the game. Guess he forgot about Coach's motto: "You start to whine, you ride the pine."

Throw yourself into the game and do your best! It's a lot more fun than sitting on the bench and complaining.

*Lord, I want to do my best for you. I know that, with your help, I can be the best person I can be for you. Thank you for loving me while I'm working on it.
Amen.*

Meditation 9

SPARKY'S DREAM

READ DANIEL 2:1-6

Snnnnrrrkkk . . . Riff! Woof! Riff! Snnnrrrkkk . . . Riff! Biff!

"Look at that crazy dog!" Thad laughed. Sparky, Thad's tubby little Daschund, lay snoozing in a sunbeam. He had rolled onto his side, and his front paws flipped out in front of his face. His round pink belly gleamed in the sun, and he was drooling on the carpet. "He must be dreaming!" Thad decided. "Look, his legs are twitching like crazy!"

Sparky was dreaming daschund dreams of chasing chipmunks and running for sticks. He barked when he dreamed of Thad feeding him little pieces of hot dog from the dinner table.

The longer the pooch slept, the funnier he acted. Before long, Thad was laughing so hard that he rolled onto Sparky. Sparky jumped up and wagged his tail at Thad. Then he trotted toward the kitchen to look for that hot dog that had seemed so real in his dream world.

Mrs. Mullet, the nasty baby-sitter who was over that day, stomped into the room. "What's this? What's this wet spot on the carpet? And what was all that racket about?"

"Sparky was dreaming," Thad answered. "It was a riot."

"Well, go on," crazy Mrs. Mullet grumbled. "Tell me what he was dreaming about. I have to tell your mom *something* when she comes home and sees you all riled up. And how am I supposed to explain this drool?"

Yep, Thad was right. Mrs. Mullet had finally blown a circuit board. She had said some crazy things to Thad before, but this one topped the list. "Guess I'll play along with her. Nothing good on TV anyway," Thad decided.

"I mean it mister, you tell me what that little sausage was dreaming about or you eat what he eats tonight—with Milk Bones for dessert!"

Crazy old Mrs. Mullet must have been some great-great-great granddaughter of Nebuchadnezzar. His demands were no less ridiculous than hers. Can you imagine being one of the king's advisors? First, the king wanted them to tell him what he had dreamed. Then they had to in-

26

terpret it! And if they couldn't, they were to be "cut into pieces" and their "houses turned into piles of rubble." Give me a Milk Bone any day.

Why was the king so upset over some dream, anyway? Well, back in Nebuchadnezzar's time, people believed that their dreams could tell them about their future. If they remembered the details of their dreams, they could consult "dream specialists"—people who could tell them what their dreams meant. Ancient Babylon's libraries were full of books on dream interpretation. And, for this dream, Nebuchadnezzar had recruited the brainiest men of the bunch.

Problem was, the king had forgotten this dream, and trying to remember it was driving him crazy. He was starting to get desperate—really desperate—because he knew the dream held some secrets about his future. That's why he called in these heavy hitters.

The wise men must have been thinking the same thing as Thad—"Okay, this time the old man has slipped. Maybe he bumped his head on the throne, or maybe that big heavy crown is too tight."

But talk about being in trouble! The king was obviously asking the impossible. On the one hand, Nebuchadnezzar was offering great rewards for the correct interpretation. But if the king *himself* didn't remember the dream, then how would he know if the magicians' interpretation was right? Their future was looking darker by the minute. How their knees must have knocked!

Tune in next time to find out what happened to those men. As for Thad, he was just sitting down to a big bowl of Alpo when his mom came home. Needless to say, crazy Mrs. Mullet was the one in the doghouse that night!

> Lord, I feel like life is unfair sometimes. Help me to know that I always can come to you for help. Thank you for always listening to me, no matter when I come to you.
> Amen.

> Meditation 10

THINK FAST!

DANIEL 2:7-15

"Young man, you get over here this instant!" Jake's neighbor yelled at him from her back porch.

Jake turned to look at Mrs. Murphy. She was shaking her bony finger at him and shouting. Her wiry gray hair was wound around mint-green rollers, and her tattered pink robe clashed with her fuzzy yellow slippers. Her snapping eyes and dark scowl told Jake he was in for it. But he didn't know why.

"I saw you digging in my garden, young man. What were you doing, stealing my strawberries? Now you listen here—I don't slave in that garden so that hoodlums like you can just waltz in and steal my fruit. It really makes me mad when blah blah blah blah. . . ."

Mrs. Murphy kept ranting and raving for about three minutes. The whole time, Jake's brain searched for an excuse. He hadn't scarfed the strawberries, but he didn't know who had, either. And Mrs. Murphy was not one to let a person off the hook easily.

"But . . . but . . ." Jake stammered. He looked at his shoes and thought about getting back at whoever had gotten him into this mess. "Mrs. Murphy, what makes you think *I* did it?"

"I saw you run off when I hollered earlier this morning, Buster, so don't deny it. I saw that red shirt when you sprinted away from me."

"Tommy!" Jake thought. He had seen Tommy earlier, wearing the same red shirt as Jake—the one with "Central Middle School" printed on the back. Both boys had blonde hair, and Mrs. Murphy couldn't see very well. "So *that's* why I'm getting nailed here," Jake groaned. He wanted to blame Tommy, but it was already too late. Mrs. Murphy had grabbed him by the ear and was hauling him back to the scene of the crime. . . .

Something similar happened to Daniel and his friends in Babylon long ago. Daniel was just sitting in his house, minding his own business, when somebody knocked on the door. The king's officer told Daniel to come with him—and not to worry about packing a toothbrush, if you know what I mean.

By order of Nebuchadnezzar, Daniel wouldn't be coming home again. The king had been so furious with the wise men for not interpreting his dream that he sentenced all of them to death.

Think of that! Being executed for something you didn't even do! But the Bible says that "Daniel spoke to him [the king's officer] with wisdom and tact." Placed in the same situation, "wisdom and tact" would be about the last thing on my mind. I'd probably be thinking about the best way to high-tail it out of the city at that point. But Daniel kept his wits about him. He trusted that God would see him through this crisis.

So Daniel held it together. Happily, so did Jake. When he and Mrs. Murphy got to the garden, Jake noticed the culprit's footprints in the dirt. "Look, Mrs. Murphy, these aren't my footprints. My feet are much bigger than this." Quick thinking, huh? How often are most people thankful for their big feet?

But Mrs. Murphy was still out for blood. Just then, Jake spotted Tommy's baseball glove under the raspberry bushes. He must have forgotten to grab it after his breakfast of strawberries.

Guess who weeded Mrs. Murphy's garden for the next month?

*Lord, every day I need your help. I do my best to stay out of trouble, but sometimes that's just not good enough. When I get into sticky situations, please give me the same wisdom that you gave to Daniel.
Amen.*

Meditation 11

BATTER UP

DANIEL 2:14-16

Ever wonder what it would be like to be a professional baseball player? I'm sure that many of you have played the game before. If not, perhaps you've watched your friends or family members play. Still, whether you're a little-league standout or a sure-fire phys ed strike-out, you probably know how the game is played.

If you're like most people, you probably look at the pros on TV and say to yourself, "Hey, that doesn't look so tough. Maybe if I practice hard, I'll be able to do that someday." And maybe, just maybe, some of you will.

But think for a minute about what being a professional baseball player requires. First of all, you've got a pitcher on the mound who is doing everything in his power to mess you up. All he wants you to do is fan away at that ball so he can go back to the dugout for another cup of Gatorade. Let's face it, pitchers have to be sly. It's their *job* to trick people.

Then you have the problem of playing your own position. I remember when I played church softball. For some unknown reason, I was elected to play catcher. Not such a difficult job when you're playing slow-pitch in a church league, right?

Think again. Things got pretty hairy in one game when a 250-pound church janitor galloped at me full speed, trying to beat the throw in from center field. Let's face it, Christian charity was not the first thing on his mind at that point. When the dust settled, I had actually caught the ball and tagged him out. I guess miracles still do happen.

On the professional level, players have a lot more riding on their performances than I did behind home plate. They can't just let themselves get lazy out there. One error could cost their team the game, and that could mean a slip in the league standings. And if a player's performance continues to fall short, he could be dropped from the roster and sent back to the minor leagues.

Well, in our passage for today, the game is in the bottom of the ninth. The king has single-handedly put the game on the line for all the wise men in Babylon. One error could mean the difference between life and death for them. And Nebuchadnezzar isn't going to accept a single, or a double, or even a triple. What he expects from his wise men is nothing less than a grand-slam home run.

These guys face no ordinary task. They need to find the right man for the job. But who? All of their efforts at interpreting Nebuchadnezzar's dream have failed. They have struck out in a big way, and they need to find a pinch-hitter who can provide that crucial clutch homer.

Who better than Daniel for the job? He certainly has the talent. Remember when we talked about his gifts earlier? His specialty was dream interpretation. Besides, unlike all the other wise men in Babylon, Daniel has his own personal trainer (God) to tell him just what that dream meant.

So the king's servant, Arioch, comes to Daniel. He informs him that the game is over for Daniel and the other wise men. "Hey, wait a minute," Daniel protests. "I haven't had my turn at the plate yet. Don't tell me I'm going to be killed because a bunch of minor-league rookies can't give Nebuchadnezzar what he wants."

When we last see Daniel, the umpire (King Nebuchadnezzar) has given him one more time at bat. He's in the on-deck circle, swinging his bat, getting ready to step up to the plate. All eyes are on him—every wise man in Babylon is counting on him to pull through. . . . Can he pull it off?

> Father, thank you for giving me opportunities to serve you by using the talents you've given me. I pray that I will be brave enough to "step up to the plate" when I get the call from you.
> Amen.

Meditation 12

WHAT ARE FRIENDS FOR?

DANIEL 2:17-18

A friend is
- someone who laughs at your jokes—no matter how stupid the punch lines are.
- someone who lets you beat him at Super Nintendo, even though he's had the game for three weeks and has zapped more aliens than you could ever dream of.
- someone who's always there to hang out with.
- someone who guards your back in phys ed so that the class bully doesn't pants you when you're running down the field.
- someone who helps you out when your science teacher picks you to tell the class about the wonders of photosynthesis—and you can't even pronounce it.
- someone who listens when you have a problem and really need to talk.

In our last meditation, we learned about how all the wise men of Babylon counted on Daniel to save them from angry King Nebuchadnezzar. But, as we see in today's passage, he didn't do it alone. He had three wonderful friends he could turn to in his time of need.

Check out today's passage again. After telling his friends about the situation, Daniel "urged them to plead for mercy from the God of heaven concerning this mystery."

Notice too *whom* Daniel asked for help. Here the writer of the book uses the Hebrew names: *Hananiah, Mishael,* and *Azariah.* It's fitting that these friends are called by their true names at this point. What Daniel asked of them had everything to do with their Hebrew heritage. He begged them to pray to God, the God of Israel, to show him the way.

Does it surprise you that Daniel was so jittery? It shouldn't. Daniel knew that his life and the lives of his three friends were on the line. Besides, the other wise men in Babylon were breathing down his neck.

If he messed up, they would probably slaughter him before Nebuchadnezzar had the chance.

So even though Daniel has come to be a "hero" to us, he was really just a regular guy who sometimes worried about his own abilities. He was a guy who got nervous and looked to his friends for support.

We all do that sometimes, don't we? We need friends we can go to when we need help, friends who will listen to our problems without making us feel stupid, friends we can trust with our deepest, darkest secrets.

Take a few minutes today to thank God for your friends. And while you're at it, ask for some help in being a better friend to others. You may not know any Daniels, but there are plenty of nervous, jittery, worried people out there who could use the friendship of one of God's children.

Jesus, when you walked on this earth, you had many wonderful friends. You were also a friend to many unpopular people. I thank you for the good friends that I have in my life. Show me when and where I can be a friend to others.
I'm ready. In your name,
Amen.

Meditation 13

PRAISE GOD!

DANIEL 2:19-23

In the last meditation Daniel and his friends were in a real pickle. Daniel had to come up with the meaning of Nebuchadnezzar's dream. And he had to tell the king what he had dreamed in the first place! None of the other wise men of Babylon had been able to do it. So Daniel placed his trust in God.

And you know what? God pulled through.

Check out verse 29 again. That very night, Daniel had a vision of Nebuchadnezzar's dream. The text suggests that Daniel was asleep. But he wasn't really dreaming. God directed Daniel's thoughts as he slept.

That's why Daniel sang this song of praise to God! He knew when he woke up that God had solved the mystery for him. He probably scribbled the details of the dream down on a note pad by his bed right away. Then he started writing the song we read in the verse for today: "He reveals deep and hidden things. He knows what lies in darkness."

That verse reminds me of something that happened to me last summer.

My wife and I were on a beautiful sandy beach on Grand Traverse Bay in northern Michigan. As I waded out into the chilly water up to my knees, I spotted a small snail, patiently inching along the floor of the bay. "Where are you going, little buddy?" I chuckled. He didn't seem to notice me so I put my big old Dutch foot right in his way. He just sat there until I moved it, and then kept slithering along.

I watched him for a few more minutes, and then it hit me: God knew where that little snail was going. God was directing the snail's slimy little path. God was looking out even for this snail, one of his smallest creatures. I was just an observer who happened to be at the right place at the right time. Had I not splashed into the water at that moment, I never would have seen this amazing little creature. But God was watching him the whole time.

God was watching out for Daniel that night so many years ago too. And God also watches over and cares for you and me—right here, right now.

Isn't it wonderful to be a child of the King of the universe?

*Holy God, thank you for knowing about everything in this world. You watch the stars and the galaxies, and you watch the tiniest snail, all at the same time. Thank you for the deep and hidden things that you choose to reveal to us every day.
Amen.*

Meditation 14

SAVED BY A STRANGER

DANIEL 2:24, 45-47

"What will I ever do?" Azmon fretted, pacing around the porch of his huge mansion. He wiped his hand over his sweaty forehead.

Inside the white marble mansion, Azmon's wife sat and stared at the tiles on the floor. "Why couldn't you have just made up a story, Azmon?" she wondered aloud. "You might have convinced him. King Nebuchadnezzar might have believed the story and your interpretation. I just can't believe that my husband and all of this will be gone. Gone. Gone."

Azmon stomped inside from the porch. He repeated what he had said a thousand times before: "Here I am, the most educated man in Babylon. The king trusted me. But how could I pull the king's dream out of his head? It's impossible. No man on earth could do that. Why is this happening to *me?*"

Nebuchadnezzar's threat haunted him. He saw the king's furious face. The shouts rang in his ears: "This is what I have firmly decided: If you do not tell me what my dream was and interpret it, I will have you cut into pieces and your houses turned into rubble!"

Right now, Azmon thought, *I would give away all my riches ... just for the smallest clue as to what the king's dream was.*

Suddenly there was a knock at the door. Azmon's stomach sank. He knew it was the king's servant Arioch, coming to take Azmon away— for good. His wife sobbed quietly and held him for a moment.

Another knock. This time louder. "Azmon! Open up!" Yes, it was Arioch. Azmon took one last long look at his wife and his home. Then he opened up the door.

"I have bad news, wise Azmon," Arioch said with a smirk.

How can he be so cruel as to mock me like this? Azmon wondered.

Arioch continued, "You are no longer the wisest man in Babylon, Azmon. A man named Daniel has discovered and interpreted the king's dream. Your former position is now his, and his friends have taken over the provinces that your friends used to govern."

Cold sweat beaded up on Azmon's back. The dream . . . someone had interpreted it? Really? Then . . . then the king must be satisfied. That could only mean . . .

The king's servant guessed what Azmon was thinking. "That's right, Azmon," Arioch said. "Your life has been spared. You will live, and your house will remain standing. But you'll have to answer to Daniel from now on. Do you hear me? The king has showered him with riches beyond belief. Hey—where are you going?"

Azmon raced back into the house. He grabbed his wife in a big bear hug. The two of them cried tears of joy. Azmon was saved! Saved!

Azmon had heard of Daniel before. He promised his wife that the very next day, he would find out where Daniel lived. Or he could just visit Daniel at the king's palace. He had to find out how Daniel had learned of the king's dream!

And just what do you think Daniel told Azmon?

Dear God, thank you for helping Daniel save the lives of all the wise men in Babylon. How happy they must have been! Help me to have the same joy in the new life that you give me through Jesus, your only Son.
I love you, Father!
Amen.

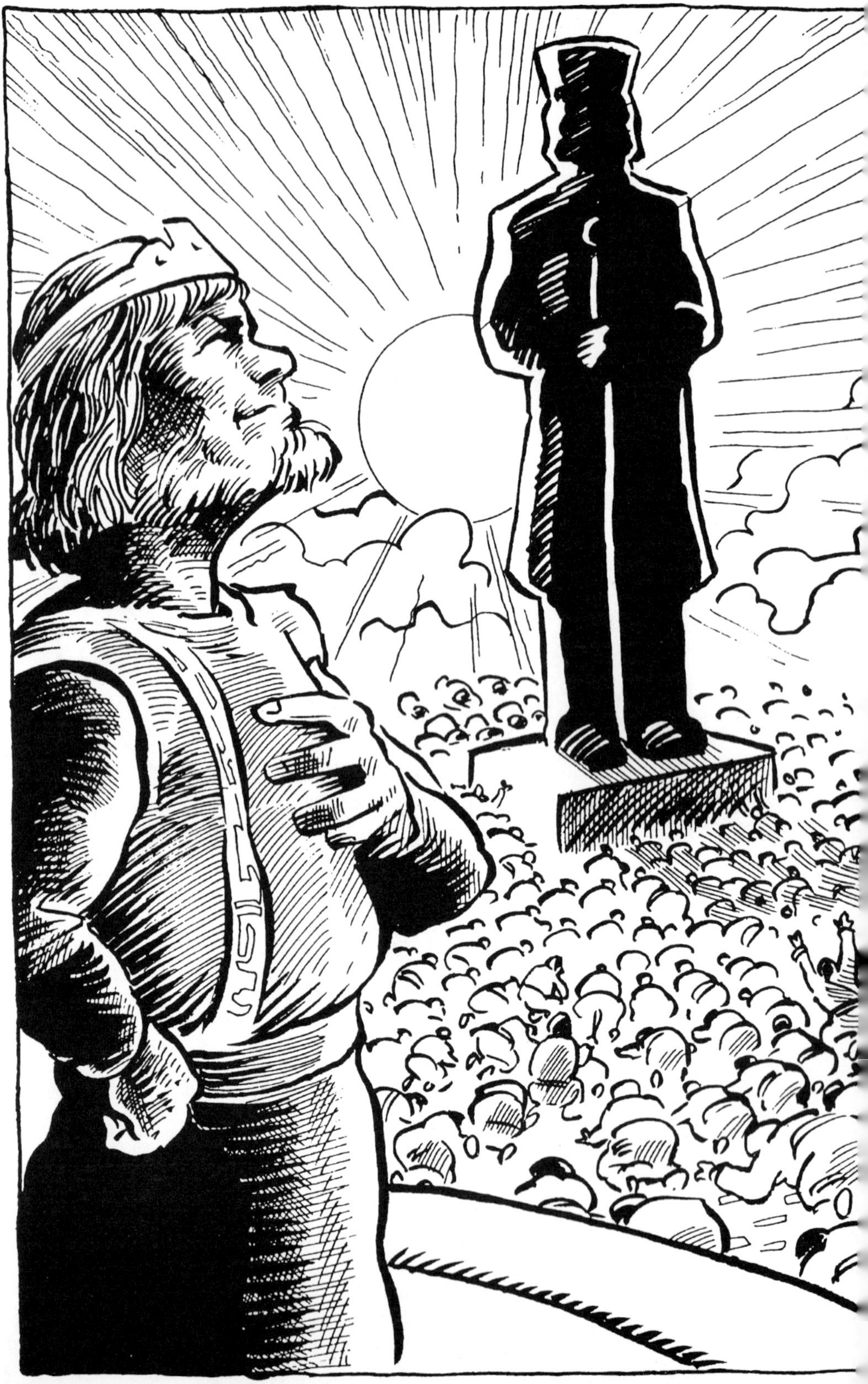

A SKINNY STATUE AND A FIERY FURNACE

Nebuchadnezzar gazed proudly at the statue he had built. The huge idol gleamed and sparkled in the sun. Satisfied with his work, the king decreed that all people must bow in worship to his idol—no exceptions allowed.

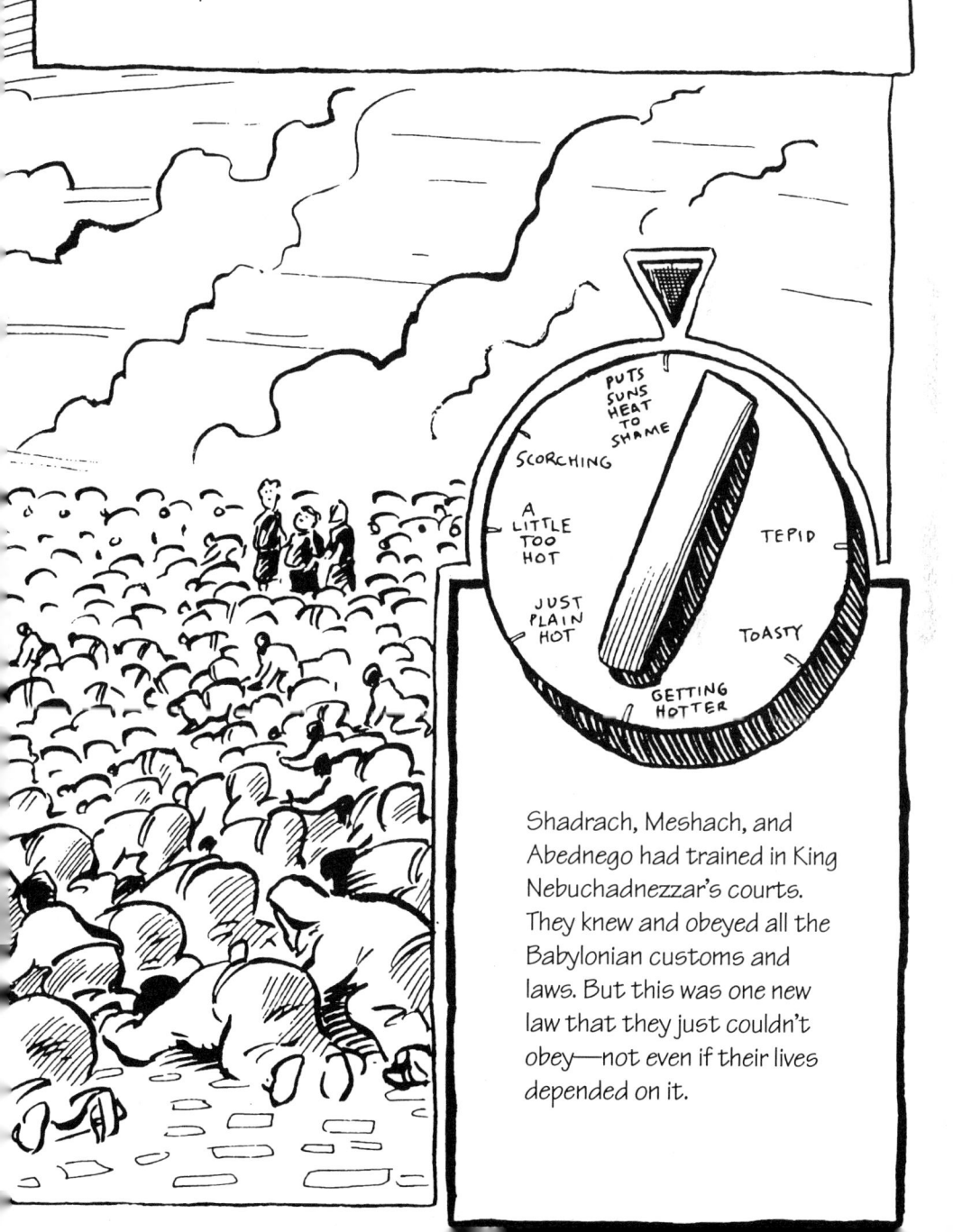

Shadrach, Meshach, and Abednego had trained in King Nebuchadnezzar's courts. They knew and obeyed all the Babylonian customs and laws. But this was one new law that they just couldn't obey—not even if their lives depended on it.

Meditation 15

PRECIOUS METAL?

READ DANIEL 3:1-6

I remember reading an old *Peanuts* comic strip many years ago. Charlie Brown is sitting at a table writing. His little sister Sally comes up behind him, holding up a piece of paper with a drawing on it. She wants her brother's attention: "Lookit this, big brother. Lookit what I drew!"

Charlie ignores her at first. "Lookit, Charlie Brown! Lookit this! Lookit! Lookit! Lookit!" Finally Charlie Brown turns and shouts, "I'M LOOKITING!"

Today's passage reminds me of that comic. King Nebuchadnezzar, fresh from his dream of a statue, decides to build one for himself. He calls all of the people of Babylon together for the grand unveiling. As he pulls the tarp off his creation, the statue gleams blindingly in the sun. The king beams with pride and says, "Lookit, people! Lookit what a great statue I made! It's pretty awesome, isn't it?"

The people eyeball the statue, then look at each other kind of strangely. "Well, sir, it's . . ." a person in the crowd speaks up, "its . . . uhhh . . . well, it's interesting." Most of the people just stare at their feet and try to figure out where the king left his brain when he got out of bed this morning.

I don't know about you, but I'm guessing that Nebuchadnezzar's statue looked pretty goofy. It was 90 feet tall (about the size of a ten-story building), but only 9 feet wide (about the size of you and your best friend laid end-to-end). If, in fact, it looked like a man, it must have looked like the skinniest, bird-leggedest, most stretched-out toothpick of a person that ever lived. And just think of the face—all long-nosed and pinchy-eyed, as homely as the day is long. How could the king be proud of this hideous thing? I think I would have fired the royal sculptor, but quick.

Actually, King Nebuchadnezzar didn't just build the statue for the fun of it. He wanted to unify the people of his kingdom by inventing one religion for everyone. See, when his people argued about which gods were real and which gods weren't, they weren't very neighborly to one another. And the people of Babylon worshiped hundreds and hundreds of different gods.

So, in order to get his people to agree on *something*, Nebuchadnezzar cooked up this idol. No doubt it was the tallest thing around, and people could see it for miles. Pretty big monument to the king, you say? Well, from the perspective of the people on the ground, I'd say you're right.

But remember, God was watching the whole time. And from God's viewpoint, that skinny statue looked pretty puny—as did the little man who ordered it built. And God was getting ready to put little King Nebuchadnezzar in his place.

God, from where you sit, even the biggest things in this world seem pretty small. Help me to remember that the next time I feel too proud of myself. And, when I have a big problem, help me to give it to you. I know you're bigger than anything this world can dish up.
Amen.

Meditation 16

BOWING TO PRESSURE

READ DANIEL 3:7

"C'mon, Tony, you can do it. Just give it a little push. It'll be hilarious. Just go ahead and do it."

Tony's buddies had set up their best stunt to date. This one even beat out the coleslaw-in-the-mall-security-guard's-face gag that they did last October. Back then, Tony was the man for the job. And today was no different.

The gang had snagged a dish of hobo pie from the cafeteria line. Just looking at it was enough to turn a person's face green. Smelling it was worse. Rumor was that Mr. Jenkins, the science teacher, wanted a sample of it to test on his lab rats. But the rats got wind of the rumor and committed suicide. Seriously—not even a prize-winning biologist could have figured out what they put in that crusty glop.

The little dish was poised on the second-floor railing, right over the vice-principal's head. Ms. Kreitzer was one of the meanest vice-principals east of the Mississippi River. She had a reputation for toughness, and right now she was chewing out a fifth-grader for running in the hall.

"Tony! Tony! Tony!" His buddies chanted softly. *Just do it, Tone*, he said to himself. *One push and you'll be a hero for another six months.* He reached out his hand and . . .

Well—you can pretty much figure out the rest. But can you figure out who's the star in this scene? If you're tempted to say Tony, think again. Tony's the sucker, not the star. He's doing exactly what his friends want him to do because he thinks he can earn popularity. Truth is, Tony's the one who's going to get burned when the heat turns up.

The people of Babylon weren't interested in popularity when King Nebuchadnezzar told them what to do. They simply wanted to avoid the king's own type of heat. He offered them a choice: either kiss the ground in front of a statue or fry in a super-hot furnace. So although they probably felt stupid, everyone—from the richest woman to the poorest beggar boy—bowed low when the music started.

From the king's point of view, the nice thing about this arrangement was that simply by asking the conductor to strike up the band, Nebuchadnezzar could prove his power over the people of his kingdom. How proud he must have felt when all the people bowed low to *his* statue! "What a bunch of suckers," the king may have snickered to himself. "They'll do anything I tell them to!"

Thankfully, none of our friends are going to threaten us with being scorched like a marshmallow if we don't do what they want. But they do sometimes threaten us in other ways. And, like Tony, we sometimes do things that we know are wrong or stupid just to avoid being mocked or left out. Think for a minute about a time when you laughed at another kid because the rest of your friends did; stole a bottle of perfume because a friend dared you to; mouthed off to an adult just to look cool. How did it feel when you got caught and/or punished?

When you think about it, it *was* kind of stupid, wasn't it? Let's face it—there's nothing tougher than standing up to people who try to make you do dumb things. But in the end, it's worth it.

You'd better believe that it wasn't Tony's *friends* who sweat it out in Kreitzer's office that afternoon. She called his father, and her tone of voice had the word "detention" written all over it. So there he was being punished, and not one of his friends had taken the fall with him. Some friends, huh?

Tony thought about that as he scraped the last few crumbs of hobo pie from the dish with his fingers. He tried to dump them under the chair, but Kreitzer glared at him. "Never, ever again," Tony muttered. He plugged his nose tightly and swallowed the last greasy mouthful.

Dear God, You weren't happy when Nebuchadnezzar made his people bow to that silly-looking statue. And you're not happy when I give in to my friends and do dumb things. Help me to look at the results of my actions before I jump in headfirst. I want to please you first of all.
In your name,
Amen.

Meditation 17

A PASSEL OF WEASELS

READ DANIEL 3:8-12

Informant. Weasel. Snitch. Tattletale. Rat. Squealer.

What pictures do these words bring to mind? I think of a shady character with shifty eyes who lurks around dark corners, waiting for other people to mess up. As soon as he overhears something bad or sees someone slip up, that person runs straight to the authorities and spills his guts.

When I was in middle school, these names meant trouble. Nobody wanted to be called a snitch. When a teacher punished someone based on details only a student could know, everyone whispered about who tattled. And when the weasel was discovered . . . well, let's just say he or she wasn't the most popular person for the next few weeks.

Sometimes the government plants people in crime organizations to gather information. When it comes to drugs and crime, we need "snitches" to put a stop to illegal activity and prevent criminals from overtaking us all. But when it comes to paper wads (teachers, please forgive me but it's true), it's probably best to keep quiet.

Speaking of snitches, have you ever read about a bigger bunch of tattlers than in today's passage? When they saw their chance, this group of astrologers squealed like a bunch of piglets all the way to Nebuchadnezzar's throne room.

"King Nebuchadneeeezzaaaarrrr," they whined, "those three guys you got to rule the local provinces aren't doing what you want them to do. When the music plays, they stand up straight as can be and pray to their own God. Remember what you said about that furnace? Well, you have your first three victims."

The fact of the matter is, those people probably didn't care one bit that Shadrach, Meshach, and Abednego didn't bow down to Nebuchadnezzar's idol. As educated astrologers, they likely thought the whole idol idea was ridiculous. But these men were next in line for the rulership positions in the provinces. Without those three pesky Hebrews around, the astrologers would be the ones in power. This was their big chance.

Remember how Shadrach, Meshach, and Abednego got their jobs? After interpreting Nebuchadnezzar's dream, Daniel was thoughtful enough to whisper a good word in the king's ear about his buddies. They climbed the government ladder right on Daniel's heels. In the process, they probably passed over their former bosses and coworkers who had been waiting for those jobs. Needless to say, these astrologers wanted them out. Permanently.

I guess the astrologers didn't know who they were messing with, did they? Remember, it was really God, not Daniel, who had given Shadrach, Meshach, and Abednego their positions of power. God was working through Daniel and his friends to protect his people. And no amount of crying to a puny king in Babylon would change God's mind.

God, your intentions for your people can't be changed by events on this earth. You know about everything that's going to happen long before things actually do. In all this, you protect people who love you. Thank you for looking out for me too. Amen.

Meditation 18

(NOT SO) TOUGH GUY

READ DANIEL 3:13-15

Dogface Dan gathered his buddies. "Here he comes, guys. You grab him, and I'll get his homework. Then we'll have another week without a math assignment." When Tim rounded the corner, Dan's two thugs grabbed him and pinned him against the wall.

"Did you finish my homework yet, you little twerp?" Dogface grabbed Tim by the collar of his sweater. He yanked little Timmy, who was half his size, close to him. Their noses almost touched as Dan got right into Tim's face.

"You . . . you're steaming up my glasses, you big baboon!" Tim protested. *Dogface,* Tim thought. *The name fits. This guy's mug is even uglier up close. Maybe they should call him "Dogbreath Dan," too.*

Normally, Tim would have been terrified. But he was used to this treatment. Whenever their math assignments were due, Dan and a couple of his goons would nab Tim in a dark corner and steal his homework. After the first week, Tim just started writing out two copies of his assignments. No, Tim wasn't afraid of Dogface anymore. He knew that he was just showing off in front of his pals. Besides, Tim knew that Dan wouldn't hurt him. With Tim in the hospital, there'd be no one around to do Dan's math homework.

The funny thing was, Tim knew that this could only go on for so long. Soon they would have a test, and Dan's assigned seat was across the room from Tim's. Long ago Mr. Rakowski had put Dan in the front row. He couldn't cheat off anybody's paper sitting right in front of the teacher's desk.

Then, Tim knew, the cat would be out of the bag. Mr. Rakowski would discover just how much old Dogface *didn't* know about math. Tim would soon be free. Mr. Rakowski would probably make Dan stay after school every day to do his math assignments under strict supervision.

Have you ever known a bully like Dan—someone who acted mean just to impress his friends or get his own way? If not, you've just met one in today's passage. In Daniel 3:4 we found out that King Nebuchadnezzar had called together "peoples, nations, and men of every language." That's a whole bunch of people, and all of them were hanging around Babylon.

So King Nebuchadnezzar had a lot of important people to impress. And when he heard that some of his own rulers were disobeying his new law, he was furious. "I'll show those wimpy Hebrews who's boss," he must have boasted to those gathered in his throne room. "Bring them to me. Watch this, guys. You're going to see some Hebrews shaking in their sandals today."

As Shadrach, Meshach, and Abednego entered the throne room, Nebuchadnezzar threatened them with the fiery furnace, as expected. To the surprise of the people who were watching, the three men kept their cool—and the king lost his, ranting and raving until his face turned red. And that's when he made his big mistake. He clenched his fists, shook them in front of the three men's faces, and roared "*I* have the power to kill all three of you! What do you think about that? WELL?"

Look at the last part of verse 15. Here Nebuchadnezzar asks, "After I toss you into my fiery furnace, 'then what god will be able to rescue you from my hand?'"

Doesn't that make you cringe? Think of how angry God must have been to hear this puny king making such threats, trying to be such a bully. King Nebuchadnezzar was saying, in effect, "I can do what I want to. And your God, whoever he is, can't stop me."

How stupid can you get? Shoot—even Dogface Dan knew better than to threaten Timmy when Mr. Rakowski was within earshot.

Lord, you rule this world and all the people in it. Sometimes people get caught up in their own power and ability, and they think they're smarter or stronger or know better than you. Help me never to make that mistake.
Amen.

Meditation 19

GRACE UNDER PRESSURE

READ DANIEL 3:16-18

Did you just read what I read? Can you believe those Hebrews? Talk about guts! Take a quick look with me around Nebuchadnezzar's throne room—just to see what's going on in this scene.

Money and power. That's all you see when you look around the room. Luxury oozes from every corner. The walls hang heavy with gold, silver, and precious jewels. So do the people. From the tips of their toes to the tops of their heads, each person—even the lowest servant—is decked out in fancy clothes. They have to be—they're in the presence of one of the world's most powerful men.

Many of the important men standing in Nebuchadnezzar's throne come from countries many miles away. Each of them has his own servants: beautiful women attendants and guards that would make Sylvester Stallone look like Pee Wee Herman. The king has summoned them to tell them about his new decree—from now on there will be one and only one religion in the empire: Nebuchadnezzar's.

In the middle of this awesome display of power stand Shadrach, Meshach, and Abednego. What are they thinking at this point? Are they afraid of the king? He is, after all, their boss. He could wipe out their futures whenever he wanted to. In fact, he has just threatened to throw them into the furnace until they're crispy-fried. Are they scared of what the king will do next?

Listen to their response:

O Nebuchadnezzar, we do not need to defend ourselves in this matter. If you throw us into the blazing furnace, the God we serve is able to save us from it, and he will rescue us from your hand, O king. But even if he does not, we want you to know, O king, that we will not serve your gods or worship the image of gold you have set up.

Well, these three Hebrews have sure showed Nebuchadnezzar, haven't they? Right in front of all these important people—some of the most powerful people in the *world*—Shadrach, Meshach, and Abednego thumb their noses at the king.

How do they dare do such an outrageous thing? These three men know where the power really is. They know because they talk to the Ruler of the universe every day. In spite of his threats, Nebuchadnezzar will never be able to hurt them because God is watching out for them. And God's care for his people will never fail.

What I really admire about Shadrach, Meshach, and Abednego is that they close off all of the king's options. Could Nebuchadnezzar hurt or kill them? Well, probably, as far as they know. But even if the king proves his power and kills them, say the three men, their God is *still* more powerful than the king.

So, just in case the fire works and the three Hebrews are reduced to ashes, Nebuchadnezzar won't have anything to brag about. He will still always know that God is more powerful than he. He'll always know that because of that powerful God, he could never get the better of these three men.

Powerful God in heaven, you give your people the freedom to trust in you. Even when times get tough, your people can rely on your strength to get them through even the stickiest situations. Help me to rely on your power at all times too. Through Jesus, Amen.

Meditation 20

SHADRACH'S STORY (PART 1)

READ DANIEL 3:19-23

Well, looks like this time we've really done it. I've never seen the king as mad as he was a few hours ago! His face changed from its normal tan to gray when we told him we wouldn't bow down to his idol. Then it turned sort of purple, and within a few minutes he was as red as a fiery desert sunset! I never thought he would get that angry at *us*, three of his best and most important rulers.

But how *could* we go along with his plan? Bowing down to his idol—aside from being just about the stupidest thing I've ever heard of—would go against our faith. Our God, the one true God of heaven and earth, has commanded that we may never bow down to idols. Long ago, God's gave his servant Moses rules for how the chosen people, the Jews, should live. Today my friends Meshach and Abednego and I still live by those rules. We know that God's word is powerful.

So when the king dragged us into his palace and demanded that we bow low to his idol, we flatly refused. Even though he has now threatened to toss the three of us into his furnace, we still refuse to bow to that skinny stick of lead that he calls a "god." Our God is much more powerful than Nebuchadnezzar or his silly-looking idol.

Will God protect us from the fire? We don't know. All we know is that we must trust in God to be with us and save us. Even dying for our God in that furnace would be a thousand times better than sniffing the dust in front of that statue.

Looks like Nebuchadnezzar is serious about killing us! To make sure our God won't be able to save us, he has stoked the fire in the furnace so it's extra hot. And here come some of the strongest soldiers in his army to tie us up!

Well, there's no question about it now. Meshach, Abednego, and I cannot possibly escape. We're tied up so tightly that we can barely even *move*, let alone free ourselves from these huge guards.

Looks like Meshach is afraid. Well, I can't blame him. My stomach is churning, too, and my heart is pounding in my ears. Who wouldn't be afraid at a time like this?

"Trust in God, Meshach. He's the only one who can get us out of this mess now." I say these words boldly to my friend, but it's so hard to believe them! Abednego is staring coldly at the fire as the guards push us toward the furnace door. Perhaps he is praying.

The heat! Even from this distance I can feel it! Black smoke is pouring out of the top of the furnace. I can see the red-hot fuel inside the furnace from here too. Strange—nobody's even standing by the furnace door. It must be too hot for anyone to go near!

The guards are crying out now as they shove us toward the furnace, and I can feel their grip loosen. The heat must really be getting to them! I wonder why the heat isn't bothering me? Maybe I can't feel it because I'm too scared. But maybe . . . maybe there's another reason. . . .

The guards give us one last push as they collapse from the heat. I've lost my balance! I'm falling into the . . . !

> Lord, Shadrach, Meshach, and Abednego went bravely into the fire, trusting that you would be with them. Their faith in you was amazing! When I suffer through bad times, help me always to look to you in faith. Though I can't see you, I know you are near.
> Amen.

Meditation 21

SHADRACH'S STORY (PART 2)

READ DANIEL 3:24-26

Falling . . . falling . . . falling—my friends and I hit the floor of the furnace hard, but all three of land on our feet.

Thinking that this is my last moment on earth, I take one final look at Meschach and Abednego. The fire rages all around us, and their faces and clothes glow red and orange like the flames. But why are they staring? Oh, look! The ropes that bound us so firmly are burning away in the fire!

We stand quietly for a few seconds, waiting for one of us to collapse. Wait—my friends are staring at me, both of them with wide-open mouths and eyes. Why? Are my clothes on fire? Is this the end of me?

No, they are both looking *past* me. I whirl around and stare, then blink hard a few times.

There—standing in the corner of the furnace—is a man! Well, at least it looks like a man. His clothes are blazing white. They're even brighter than the brightest flames in the furnace. I can't believe it—it must be God's angel, sent to protect us!

"Don't be afraid," the angel says. His voice calms us. "You will be all right. The three of you will walk out of this furnace unharmed."

"But how can it be?" Meschach blurts out. I remember his fear of a few moments ago.

"Once again I tell you, fear not!" The angel frowns at Meschach, but then his expression softens. "You have been faithful to the one true God of heaven and earth. He has seen you stand in front of Nebuchadnezzar, defending him before all those gathered in the palace. He has also heard your silent cries for help. You will be spared. God still has work for you to do for him in Babylon."

I turn and face my friends again. Still frightened, we meet in the middle of the furnace and touch each other's clothes. Can this be real? Can we be walking about in the middle of this fire and not be harmed? Abednego smiles and wraps his arms around both of our necks. "I knew God would help us, my friends!" Abednego shouts. "I just knew it!" So he *was* praying a few minutes ago as he stared at the furnace!

The angel joins our group and lays a brilliant hand on Abednego's shoulder. For the first time, the angel smiles. "You will see even more wonderful things today, children of God," the angel promises. "Yes, for even now the king of Babylon is looking into the furnace. Walk around—don't huddle together. Show him that the three of you are all right, and that the God of heaven and earth is more powerful than he can even imagine. Walk, I tell you."

We obey the angel. And a few minutes later we hear a voice: "Shadrach! Meshach! Abednego! You three servants of the Most High God, come out! Come here!"

Why, that's Nebuchadnezzar—the king of Babylon himself! The three of us glance at each other and then look for the angel. He's gone—vanished! And yet we're still safe in the flames. Smiling, the three of us make our way toward the door—the same door we just came through. Look, the guards who pushed us in lie dead on the ground. But the flames haven't touched us.

I follow Meshach and Abednego through the door. We don't care that the king of Babylon is waiting to see us—it's time to celebrate. We hug each other tightly. All three of us shed tears of joy as we praise God together.

"Praise to you, O God! Praise to the great King of heaven and earth!"

> Lord, I praise you for your power today—
> just as Shadrach, Meshach, and Abednego did
> many years ago. You rule the earth and watch over
> us, and you do both things with your
> loving hand. Thank you!
> Amen.

Meditation 22

SHADRACH'S STORY (PART 3)

READ DANIEL 53:15, 27-30

Free! We're free from that awful furnace!

I bury my face in Meshach's shoulder. Abednego throws his arms around both of us, and we laugh together. But wait . . . what's this? Meshach's clothes don't smell like smoke! They smell clean, as if they have just been washed. How about Abednego? His clothes look the same. There's not a trace of soot on him—not even on his sandals! But that's impossible. How can it be?

And look at me! Not a single thread on my cloak is singed. And my clothes smell clean too—fresher than they did when I put them on this morning! Oh, what a great God we have—he has delivered us from death, and has protected us even to the point of saving our *clothes* from the fire. It's as if we'd never even been near to that terrible furnace!

We approach Nebuchadnezzar with a spring in our steps. My face aches from smiling! But I must observe the proper code for addressing the king of Babylon. Stop smiling Shadrach! Show proper respect!

Wait a second—why in the world should I be serious and respectful to this man? Who is he but just another man, another person on this earth? Forget it! I can't help myself—after seeing the brightness of God's angel, this "great king" looks like a beggar. Praise God! Praise the Lord for his power!

All the great men who were in the throne room this morning wait with Nebuchadnezzar now, staring at us in amazement. All the satraps, prefects, governors, and royal advisors are here, too. And look—there are the men who told the king about us in the first place! Ha! They see me looking at them, and they're walking away like they're in a big hurry to get somewhere. I guess I'd run if I were them too.

"What in the world happened in there?" "Who was that man with you?" "How did you escape?" The royal advisors have so many questions that we can't even begin to answer them all.

Then the crowd quiets; Nebuchadnezzar wants to talk. Unlike these other so-called wise men, he doesn't ask us what went on in the fiery furnace. He saw what happened firsthand. He knows that God has met his challenge. What was that he said earlier today? Wasn't it, "Then what god will be able to deliver you from my hand?" Well, now he has his answer!

The king of Babylon fingers the sleeve of my cloak. He sniffs around Abednego's shoulder. He examines Meshach's sandals. And he doesn't find a trace of soot or smoke anywhere! Then the great Nebuchadnezzar turns and says,

"Praise be to the God of Shadrach, Meshach, and Abednego, who has sent his angel and rescued his servants! These men trusted in their God, and were willing to die rather than displease him. Therefore I decree, in the presence of all of you rulers and citizens, that if anyone says anything against the God of Shadrach, Meshach, and Abednego, they will surely be killed and their houses destroyed. Is that clear?"

The people turn away. Nobody would ever dare question *this* decree from Nebuchadnezzar. All the rulers, even those from other lands, nod in agreement. They too have seen the power of our great God.

How wonderful! The angel promised we would see amazing things today. Nebuchadnezzar's decree isn't as exciting as walking out of the fiery furnace, but it is no less amazing. Praise be to the Lord!

God, you proved your power, and you changed Nebuchadnezzar's heart. At that time, some of the most important people of the world witnessed your power and believed in you. Help me to remember to tell others of your strength and to believe in you with all my heart.
Amen.

KING NEBUCHADNEZZAR LEARNS A BEASTLY LESSON

King Nebuchadnezzar was the most powerful king in the world. As he looked over his kingdom, he figured he had it all. What other king had more wealth or power than he did? Nebuchadnezzar couldn't think of any, and his chest swelled with pride.

As far as God was concerned, however, this earthly king was in sad shape. Nebuchadnezzar had ignored Daniel's advice to turn from sin. Now it was time for Nebuchadnezzar to learn who held real power in the world. God was going to teach the king of Babylon a lesson that he would never forget.

Meditation 23

GOOD ADVICE

READ DANIEL 4:24-27

What advice have you heard lately?

When I was your age, my mom and dad had all kinds of good advice for me. Most of it had to do with how to live with others and how to be a good person. They showed me the importance of following God, of worshiping him and loving his Son Jesus. They taught me lots of other things, too, that helped me both then and now—although some of them sounded kind of crazy at the time. Perhaps you've heard a few of these yourself. I've placed them in different categories for your convenience:

- *Kindness:* "Don't hit your sisters." This seemed really stupid at the time. I mean, when your older sisters pinch you, pin you down, swish their long hair in your face, and tickle you to within an inch of your life, you have to defend yourself, right? My sisters bugged me, so why *not* hit them? I always hit my twin brother when he bothered me and nobody said a word. But this advice set my sisters apart in my mind. I learned that when you treat others with kindness, you get kindness in return.

- *Courtesy:* "Take your shoes off outside." This advice was basically given in self-defense. My brother and I had four of the stinkiest, most putrid feet on the block. In order avoid a costly investment in gas masks, my parents asked us to respect the rest of the family by leaving our shoes in the garage. This advice helped me consider the results of my actions *before* I did something that would affect other people.

- *Responsibility:* "Feed the dog, and take her for a walk." Now, I sometimes wonder if our dog might have preferred just sitting in the kitchen looking for a handout instead of walking on a scorching summer day or a frozen winter morning. But this advice taught me to be responsible for certain things. I discovered that if I didn't take care of them, bad things would happen.

- *Just Plain Good for You:* "No dessert until you've cleaned your plate." Always popular with parents, this advice kept me well nourished and helped me grow into a person who is now six-foot-two and two hundred pounds. Problem is, now I clean my wife's plate too.

Perhaps after reading this meditation you'll say to yourself, *Well, I don't care if that advice worked for you—after all, you're an adult too!* And that's true. Fact is, I'd like to use some of my parents' advice on my own kids someday. I've lived long enough to see the results of their advice, and I know what works and what doesn't.

But the best advice I can give to you today comes straight from Daniel. Daniel told Nebuchadnezzar, "Renounce your sins by doing what is right." That's basically the same advice my parents gave me. Do what is right in the sight of your family. Do what is right in the sight of your Christian friends. And, most important, do what is right in the sight of God.

This is what God says to you and me in the book of Proverbs: "The fear of the LORD is the beginning of wisdom, and knowledge of the Holy One is understanding. . . . If you are wise, your wisdom will reward you; if you are a mocker, you alone will suffer."

That's good advice. In fact, it's probably the best advice you'll ever hear. Fear God. Be wise. And live a happy life.

Dear Lord, following your advice is the best thing I can do. Help me to do what is right in your sight—all day, every day.
Amen.

Meditation 24

THE PROBLEM WITH PRIDE

READ DANIEL 4:28-32

The last meditation mentioned that Daniel advised Nebuchadnezzar to turn from his wickedness and do what is right in the sight of God. This advice came on the heels of one of the king's dreams. As he did after his last confusing dream, Nebuchadnezzar asked Daniel for an interpretation. God blessed Daniel by revealing the meaning of the dream, and Daniel relayed the interpretation to the king.

To put it in a nutshell, things didn't look good for Nebuchadnezzar. Daniel told him he would be thrown out of the kingdom and that he'd be eating grass salads (we're talking dandelions instead of croutons, here) for a long time—at least until he shaped up. All this would happen unless the king cleaned up his act and did what was right in God's eyes.

Well, for a year it seemed to work. Daniel's frightening prediction didn't come to pass, and all was well . . . until one day when Nebuchadnezzar lost his perspective.

Yep, the king was feeling pretty good about himself that day. Can you picture him? He walks out on the roof of his palace on a bright sunny morning. A cool breeze is blowing, and the city sparkles in the sunlight. He's had a good night's sleep last night, he's just polished off a delicious breakfast, and his pesky advisors haven't started bugging him yet. It's enough to make anyone feel pretty good.

But Nebuchadnezzar pushes it too far, saying to himself, "Is this not the great Babylon I have built as the royal residence, by my power and by the glory of my majesty?" Pride in himself and in his accomplishments oozes from his ears, and he forgets the God who placed him there and who is responsible for everything he is and does.

Not that Nebuchadnezzar believed in God necessarily. As we have seen before, Babylon was filled with many gods and religions. The God of Daniel was only one of many that the king had heard of. While we'll find out later that he *does* come to realize the true God's power, at this point he is too wrapped up in himself to recognize who's really in control.

But not for long. Before the last word of his sentence leaves his mouth, God thunders down at him. Nebuchadnezzar had forgotten Daniel's prediction and needed a reminder. So God again tells the king that his royal position has been taken away from him. He will live like an animal until he realizes that there is a God in heaven who claims his loyalty.

Poor King Nebuchadnezzar had a problem: he was so wrapped up in his own affairs that he had forgotten about God. You might wonder how the king could do such a thing. If somebody warned *you* that if you were too proud, you would lose your grip on reality and act like an animal, you'd remember to stay away from the sin of pride, right?

The fact is, it's really not so hard to fall into the same sin that Nebuchadnezzar committed. Most of us do it every single day. When we take all the credit for doing well on a test, or for scoring a hat trick in the hockey game, or for helping the church janitor paint a stairwell, we run into a problem with pride. We lose our perspective on who's in control and who deserves the real credit.

God offers us the opportunity to shine, to succeed at what we do best. God wouldn't give us talents if he didn't want us to use them. But instead of getting a big head about our accomplishments, we need to give credit where it is due—to the one who loves us and who gives us talents in the first place.

Dear God, help me to see that all I have is from you, and that all I am able to do is a gift from your hand. Thank you for letting me use these gifts for your glory. In Jesus' name, Amen.

> **Meditation 25**

THE REAL WOLF-MAN

READ DANIEL 4:33

In the darkness of a misty midnight, another unsuspecting victim strolls the streets of London. Walking quickly, for the streets are dangerous, he peers around him. The full moon glows greenish in the fog and casts an eerie light on the cobblestone street.

What was that? Did something growl? The young man quickens his step. *Only four more blocks to go,* he thinks, *then I'll be safe in my own home.*

Rounding the last corner, he hears a dog running behind him. But this is no ordinary dog. This is a wolf—and this wolf used to be a *man.* Just as the young man reaches the steps of his townhouse, he turns to see the snarling wolf-man pounce! Too scared to scream, he covers himself. But it's too late. . . .

Hollywood. How many times haven't we seen movies or TV shows about people turning into wolves under the full moon? Legend has it that such wolf-people really exist, and movie producers' active imaginations have been giving the film-going public nightmares for decades.

Those silver screen images are nothing more than plastic-fanged phonies, covered with fake fur and industrial-strength glue. But today's passage introduces a *real* wolf-man—probably the only one in history. The writer of Daniel tells us that God's words immediately came true, and King Nebuchadnezzar lost his mind. Although he didn't grow fur and claws right away, he *was* instantly changed from a powerful king into a grunting, grass-eating outcast.

Not that he roamed the streets looking for victims, as do those Hollywood hairballs. The Bible tells us that he was a peaceful wolf-man and that he lived out in the fields with the cattle. There he spent his days getting "drenched with the dew of heaven until his hair grew like the feathers of an eagle and his nails like the claws of a bird." Sounds like several heavy-metal headbangers I've seen recently on posters at the music store.

Taking away Nebuchadnezzar's sanity was God's way of dealing with the former king's pride. Remember in the last meditation, how puffed up the king's cranium was? I'll bet he wasn't so proud of himself as he competed for the juiciest grasses with his cow-faced cronies. God wanted to put Nebuchadnezzar in his place, to make him realize who had given him his kingly position. And, although it would take a while, the king would eventually come around.

So that's the story of the Bible's first recorded wolf-man. But what about the legend that still exists today—could it really be true? Come to think of it, my little daschund Gretel always did act a little weird when the full moon was out. And you should have seen my brother wolf down a plate of spaghetti! Face full of pasta, tomato sauce flying, doggie running in circles around the kitchen—Hmmm . . . maybe there's something to that legend, after all.

Nah.

Dear God, you used unusual methods to show King Nebuchadnezzar who was the real ruler of this world. You show me your power through creation and through your Word. Thank you for showing me your power and love. Amen.

Meditation 26

SHAVE AND A HAIRCUT...

READ DANIEL 4:34-37

Not too long ago I got my monthly shearing. Only it had been about six weeks. Needless to say, I desperately needed a haircut. When I walked in, I asked the woman who usually cuts my hair if she would help me out by cutting the bush off my head. She replied, "Bush? Why, I thought that was a *cat* sleeping on your head!"

I gave her a big tip that night—extra credit for imagination. But I'll bet my thick mop was nothing compared to Nebuchadnezzar's shaggy mane by the time he came to his senses.

So how did the king regain his sanity? Through the writer of Daniel, the king tells us that "I raised my eyes toward heaven, and my sanity was restored." Amazing, isn't it? In an instant, Nebuchadnezzar realized who he was, what his place was in creation, and who had given him his position in the first place. It's as if God said, "O.K., little man. I guess you've done your time. Now I will restore you to your throne." Never skipping a beat, Nebuchadnezzar "praised the Most High." He "honored and glorified him who lives forever."

Reread Nebuchadnezzar's words in verses 35 and 37. Does this sound like a changed man to you? Seems as if the king had learned his lesson. The greatest evidence that his pride had fallen comes in his last words in the chapter: "Those who walk in pride he is able to humble."

So how did the king let his subjects know that he was back in business? First of all, he would have had to make himself presentable. Imagine the king shuffling back on to Main Street in Babylon and heading to the barber shop for a shave and a haircut:

"Hey, Barney—what d'you suppose *that is?*"

"I dunno, Lester. Looks like one of them there hippie freaks to me. Hope he stays outta here.... Nope, here he comes."

"Hey, mister, what you want? I run a clean place here, and you (sniff), you ain't nowhere near clean."

"Listen to me, you backwoods hayseed. I am your great king, King Nebuchadnezzar. I regained my sanity and have returned to Babylon to reclaim my throne."

"Yeah, right, and I'm the Sultan of Syria. Getta load of this guy, Barney!"

Well, the Bible tells us that *someone* must have recognized Nebuchadnezzar when he entered the city. We read that his nobles "sought him out," and he was restored to his throne.

After his bout with insanity, the king must have had a new perspective on life in general. Because of his brand-spanking-new attitude, the Lord blessed him in his position. He became even greater and more powerful than he had ever been before.

This is the last we'll see of our old buddy Nebuchadnezzar. Commentators doubt whether this king ever had a truly personal relationship with God. But just look at how God affected his life! Whatever his attitude toward God, after this experience Nebuchadnezzar was never the same.

God has that effect on people, doesn't he?

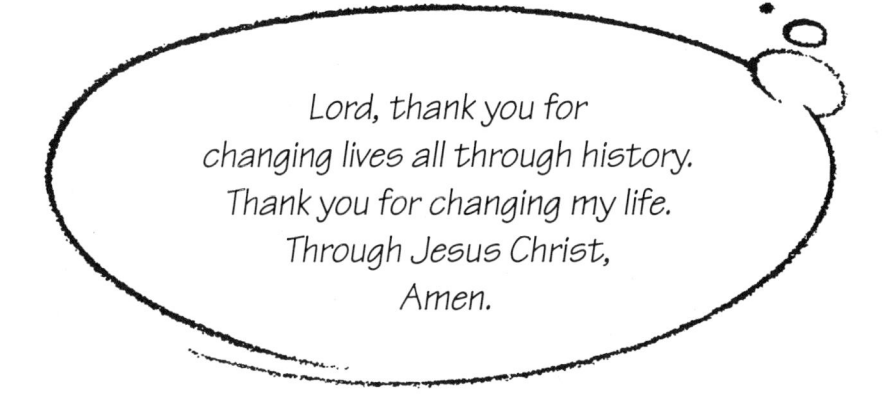

> Lord, thank you for
> changing lives all through history.
> Thank you for changing my life.
> Through Jesus Christ,
> Amen.

DIVINE GRAFFITI

Perhaps you've seen graffiti before—words spray-painted in different colors on the sides of buildings. Whoever paints those words breaks the law to get his or her message across. Such people apparently want their message to be seen and read by everyone who cares to look.

God had the same intention when he wrote on the wall in Belshazzar's palace. But he didn't use red or green or blue spray-paint—he used his finger. And his message wasn't for everyone—it was for Belshazzar alone. When God wrote on the wall, he broke the normal rules of this world by revealing himself in physical form. But that's O.K. After all, God sets the rules in the first place, right?

Meditation 27

HOW CAN YOU PARTY AT A TIME LIKE THIS?

READ DANIEL 5:1-4

When the vase shattered, Jimmy knew he was in trouble. The glass lay scattered in tiny pieces all over the family room. He had meant to be careful with his new tennis racket. But he hadn't figured on *this* kind of a backhand smash.

"I *knew* I should have gone outside with this thing!" Jimmy scolded himself. But he knew his own words were nothing compared to the scolding his mother would deliver in a few seconds. He started to pick up the glass. "Maybe she didn't hear it," he muttered hopefully. "Maybe she won't . . . "

"Jimmy?" His mother called from the basement. "Did I hear something break up there? Are you okay?"

"Yeah, Mom," Jimmy called back. "Just had a little, um, accident here."

What kinds of things do you do when you're in trouble? Do you hide in your room? Escape to a friend's house? Hurry outside to walk the dog?

How about having a party? That's right, a party. Does that sound like a good idea when you're in hot water up to your eyeballs?

That's what King Belshazzar does in today's story. But before we talk about that story, you may be wondering what happened to Nebuchadnezzar. Truth is, the writer of Daniel doesn't say. After the king's final speech at the end of Daniel 4, we never hear from him again.

In today's passage Belshazzar is called the "son" of Nebuchadnezzar, but he really isn't the king's child. He's actually a distant relative of the old king who somehow, some way, found his way to the throne of Babylon.

Too bad he didn't inherit a few of Nebuchadnezzar's brains. When we first meet Belshazzar, he's ordering a wonderful feast for himself and a thousand nobles. Now, normally that wouldn't be so bad. After all, if you were a rich ruler, wouldn't you want to throw a huge pizza party for a thousand of your friends?

Problem is, standing right outside the city gates are the armies of his enemy, King Darius. And Darius definitely isn't on the guest list for this party. Darius has other plans for Babylon, and King Belshazzar knows that he and his Babylonian army are about to be run out of town.

Belshazzar wants to forget about his troubles, so he orders Babylon's finest meats, cheeses, and wines for this great and final feast. He also orders some golden goblets to be taken out of storage and polished. Now, these aren't just any old goblets from the marketplace. These are the goblets that the Babylonians had stolen from the temple in Jerusalem decades earlier.

You thought Belshazzar was in hot water from Darius? Well, just you wait and see what happened when he used those special goblets to worship idols!

Father, you help me to know what's right and what's wrong. Thank you that I know enough to steer clear of trouble. And when I do mess up, help me to know how to act in a way that pleases you most. Amen.

Meditation 28

GOD'S FINGER

READ DANIEL 5:4-9

When we left Belshazzar, he was raising a big goblet of wine to one of his favorite idols. But that goblet was once used for another purpose—worshiping the true God of Israel.

God knew what was going on in Babylon. He had been watching Darius build up armies outside the city. He knew what was going to happen to Belshazzar. So when the drunken king lifted this special goblet in worship of a false god, our God decided to shake things up a bit.

As the king sat drinking wine and impressing all his fine friends, something caught the corner of his eye. He turned to look and saw the fingers of a human hand floating in midair! Those fingers touched the white plaster wall and mysteriously scratched out a message for Belshazzar.

The king's face turned a ghostly white. The room quieted, and the guests watched Belshazzar's knees knock. His legs failed him, and he collapsed.

Well, can you blame the king for freaking out a little bit? Remember, this was ancient Babylon. Special effects hadn't been invented yet. King Belshazzar had never even *heard* of a movie theater, let alone Stephen Spielberg. This was no fake prop, no computer-animated cartoon. This was the *real thing*.

The king knew this was a divine message for him, but he couldn't understand what it meant. His instincts told him that the message was telling him something about his future. But what did these words mean? He called all of his wise men together to solve the mystery. He just *had* to know what that eerie hand had written! He *had* to learn what the future held!

God doesn't leave us messages like that today. Occasionally we wish he would. Don't you sometimes wish you knew whether a particular boy or girl liked you? Don't you wish you knew whether you'd get the part you tried out for or make the team?

Well, you're not alone. Many adults wish they knew what the future holds too. They wonder whom they will marry. They wonder where their next job will be and where their family will live. As they get older, they wonder if they'll become sick or have to move out of their home. Perhaps your parents can tell you what they wonder about the most.

No, God doesn't write on walls today. But he does give us the Bible and other people to let us know what he wants us to do. When we read God's Word and listen to people who love God, we can hear God speak.

Wondering what the future holds for you? God knows. In fact, God knows everything that's going to happen to you every single day for the rest of your life. Read God's Word. Listen to the advice of Christians you know and respect. Then live in peace, knowing that God will be with you every single step of the way. The future is nothing to worry about—God's already there.

> *Father in heaven, you know what my life holds for me. But I usually find it hard to look past what will happen after lunch. Thank you for watching out for me.*
> *In Jesus' name,*
> *Amen.*

Meditation 29

DANIEL TO THE RESCUE

READ DANIEL 5:10-17

"Bonjour, class! Aujourd'hui nous conmmencons une nouvelle classe de Français. Dans cette classe, nous ne parlons jamais d'Anglais. C'est bien, oui? Oui."

So began one of the scariest high school classes I ever took. Here was a woman speaking to me in a language I had never heard before, except for when my older sisters recited their lessons. I took the class because I didn't have to buy the books, having received them from those same older sisters. What my teacher had said was that throughout this class, we wouldn't speak a word of English.

"What am I doing in here?" I thought to myself. My brother had enrolled in Spanish classes with some of our friends. He had an advantage going into that class; he knew some of the basic Spanish vocabulary. He had learned a few words from watching *Sesame Street* as a little kid.

Okay, so maybe he wasn't ready to travel to Mexico just yet, but he could at least count to ten in Spanish. Besides, he had the whole Taco Bell menu to back him up. If the teacher asked him a question and he didn't know the answer, he could just smile and say, *"Si. Nachos Bell Grande mi burrito y enchilada."*

The only French words I knew were "french bread" and "french fries." And I wasn't even sure those were really French! I knew right then and there I needed a tutor—someone to interpret this strange language for me.

But I wasn't anywhere near as frightened in that class as Belshazzar was in his throne room. My semester grades would be affected by my success in the class, but the king of Babylon's entire *future* was on the line. Besides, my teacher was a real human being, not some eerie hand carving words into the plaster. Belshazzar needed an interpreter in the worst way. But none could be found among the wise men in his palace.

It's been quite a while since we've heard from Daniel. You remember Daniel, the man of God who could interpret dreams? The one whom this book is written about?

As it turns out, interpreting dreams wasn't his only talent. Today's passage tells us he was also widely known as one of the world's best language interpreters. But, as we shall see, Daniel never took credit for these talents. He always made it clear that his talents came straight from God.

Once again, Daniel's reputation followed him. If you'll remember, the last time he was called into the throne room, it was because Nebuchadnezzar couldn't figure out a dream. The queen in today's story remembered Daniel's work. She recalled that Daniel's words had come true. That's why she told Belshazzar to find him: "Call for Daniel, and he will tell you what the writing means." Must have been nice for Daniel to be so well known for his wits.

As he stood in Belshazzar's throne room, Daniel played it straight. He refused to accept the king's riches—the word of God could not be bought with the promise of a bag of gold and a purple robe. Setting his jaw firmly, Daniel prepared to give Belshazzar the interpretation he was after. . . .

> Lord, thank you again for the talents that you gave Daniel. We thank you that you used him to speak to kings on your behalf. We ask that we, too, may be happy to use our talents for your glory.
> Amen.

73

Meditation 30

THE INTERPRETATION

READ DANIEL 5:18-30

Daniel's interpretation of the king's dream can be summarized as follows:

*"O King Belshazzar, as you sit on your bench
you sweat and you shake and your teeth tightly clench.
You've been spoken to harshly by God, heaven's King
who rules over earth and each living thing.*

*"This is the God who gave glory and splendor
to the previous ruler—King Nebuchadnezzar.
So great was this monarch that all bowed in fear
whenever King Nebbie was anywhere near.*

*"One day when this king thought about Babylon
he smiled and he whooped and he bragged on and on
about how great was the land and how great was he
who had built up this kingdom from sea to sea.*

*"This would have been fine if this proud old guy
had praised to true God in heaven's sky.
For God was the one who had given him power,
and God spoke to the king in that very hour.*

*"'Because of your pride, little man,' declared God,
'You will live like a beast in the fields eating sod.
Your hair will grow long, and you'll grow claws too,
and your back will be drenched in the morning with dew.'*

*"For seven whole years, the king roamed around
in the fields like the cattle, eating stuff off the ground.
His sanity left him, his hair and nails grew,
and he lived with the beasts—what God said came true.*

"In time the old king regained his reason
and praised the true God who directs every season.
He humbled himself in the sight of the Lord
and commanded his subject to remember God's word.

"But you, Belshazzar, though you knew this fable
have rejected God's word. You have sat at your table
drinking wine out of goblets from Jerusalem—
you've sacrificed to idols as guzzled from them.

"As you've prayed to your idols made of gold, wood, and stone
you've completely denied God's heavenly throne.
Can't you see that this God, who possesses all power,
holds your life in his hand at this very hour?

"That's why the hand that gave you a fright
wrote Mene, Tekel, Parsin on the wall last night.
Those words, as you guessed, were meant for your nation
and to me God has given the interpretation.

"God's been watching your reign and your wicked ways.
Because of your sin, he will number your days.
Listen up, O king, listen up, all his friends,
Belshazzar has failed. His reign will now end!

"The Medes and the Persians by the city walls wait.
Tonight they will crash great Babylon's gate.
Leaving death and destruction, they'll strike once and again,
and you, Belshazzar, will surely be slain."

These words Daniel spoke as the messenger of heaven,
and the king soon saw that the truth had been given.
God's judgment came to pass on that night, so we read,
and Babylon fell to Darius the Mede.

We can all learn a lesson from the story we heard:
we must all listen up and heed our God's Word.
"Pride goes before a fall"—yes, the old saying's true,
so be humble to God in all that you do.

> Heavenly Father, as you held Belshazzar's life in your hand, so you hold my own. Thank you that I can rest easy in that knowledge. And when you speak, help me to listen.
> Amen.

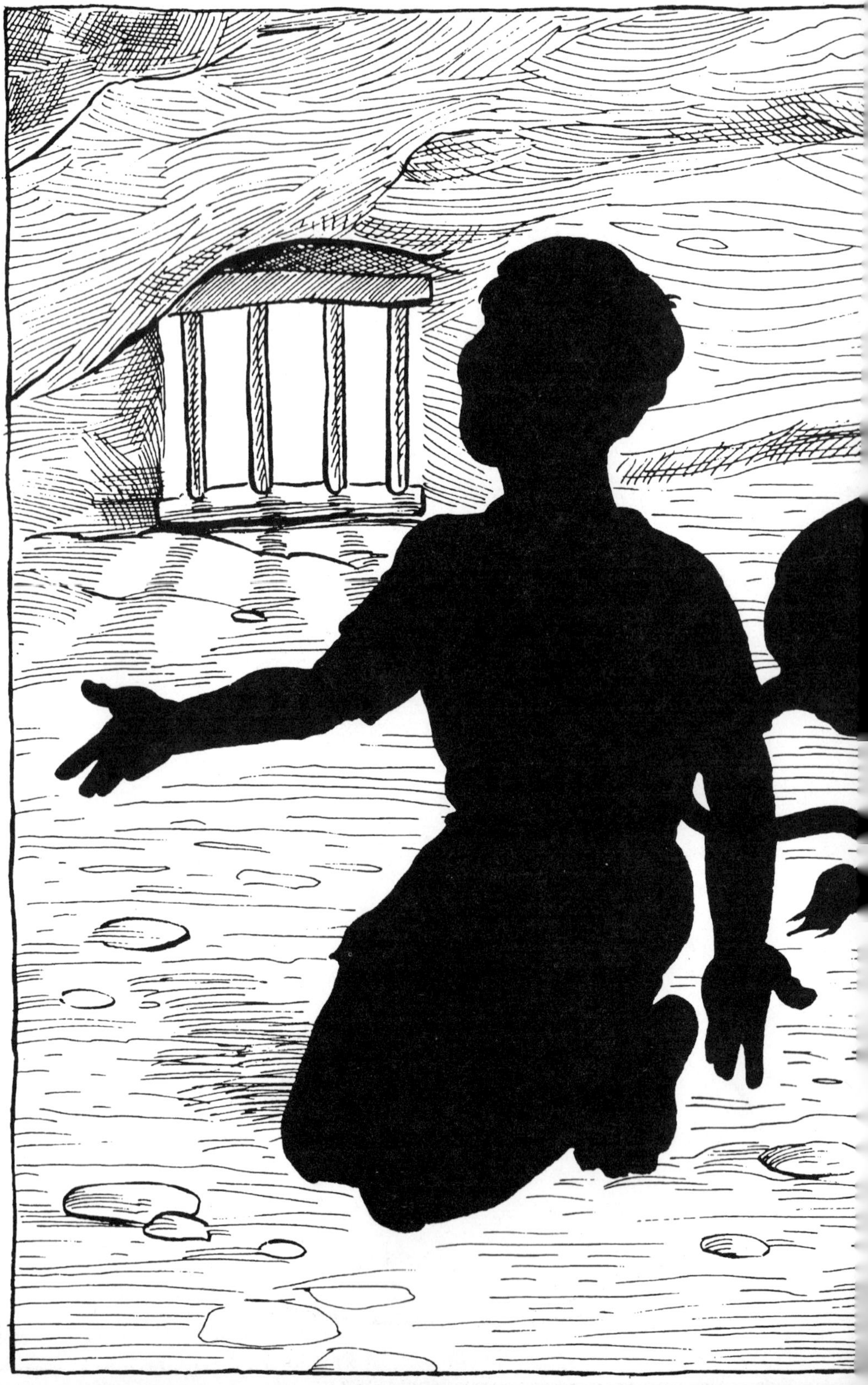

DANIEL'S NIGHT WITH THE BIG CATS

The last story in this book is one of the best-known stories in the Bible. It contains all the elements of a good novel: a powerful, proud ruler; his evil, back-stabbing advisors; a good man who is unfairly accused; a thrilling action scene; and a happy ending (for Daniel, that is). In this story, Daniel puts his life on the line. He would rather brave the teeth and claws of hungry lions than betray his God. He knows God is much stronger than the big cats and much more powerful than King Darius. As you read the following meditations about the story and Daniel's own account, look for ways to show the same trust in God.

Meditation 31

KINGDOM RESPONSIBILITIES

READ DANIEL 6:1-3

Do you remember the story of King Midas, the greedy old ruler? When he was granted one wish, Midas asked that everything he touched would turn to gold. That may *sound* great, but Midas soon discovered that his new talent brought him plenty of trouble. He couldn't eat, because as soon as his teeth bit into a piece of fruit, it turned to solid gold. He couldn't sleep, because the minute he lay down on his bed, the soft, downy sheets and blankets turned into a stiff, crinkly gold foil. He was miserable!

In today's culture we've forgotten how miserable King Midas was. We've turned this negative story into a positive one. We say of someone who has repeated successes that he or she has "the Midas touch" (no, I don't mean the muffler company). It seems like everything these people do turns out right, no matter how many risks they take or how hard (or how little) they work.

Do you know anybody like that? Do some kids in your class always get A's on their homework—seemingly without working hard at all? Do some people in your phys ed class always get base hits in softball and always score the most points in hoops without breaking a sweat? Or perhaps you're one of these naturally talented individuals. If so, good for you!

It's obvious from today's passage that Daniel had what we would call "the Midas touch." Even though the kingdom of Babylon fell to the Medes and the Persians, Daniel still remained at the top of his game. The passage tells us that "Daniel so distinguished himself among the administrators and the satraps by his exceptional qualities that the king planned to set him over the whole kingdom" (Dan. 6:3).

Wow! What a wonderful distinction. History tells us that Daniel earned his position by being an upright, law-abiding citizen. He had proved his worth as an administrator during the reign of Nebuchadnezzar, back when he was a young man. Now that he was old, the years of listening to his Lord and being an efficient and effective servant for the government had served him well. Daniel was extremely wise, and King Darius knew it. He planned to use Daniel to help him govern the Persian Empire, largest kingdom the world had ever known.

Each of us has an important task in this world too. We live on God's earth as members of God's kingdom. Like Daniel, we must care for God's kingdom in all that we do. God wants us to look after creation, using all the talents we have been blessed with.

Don't you want to be like Daniel? Don't you want to have the distinction of being someone whom God, the true King of the universe, can use for the benefit of his kingdom? Wouldn't you like to "so distinguish" yourself in front of God that you are seen as having "exceptional qualities" for use in God's service?

That's what God requires of all of us. In small ways (recycling a tin can) and large ways (starting a recycling program at your school), we can all care for God's kingdom. Although you may not have "the Midas touch" as far as schoolwork and sports are concerned, your care for God's creation can turn your efforts into gold for God's kingdom!

*Lord, you gave Daniel important work to do for you, and you blessed the work of his hands. As we try to do your will, bless the work we do for you too.
In Jesus' name,
Amen.*

Meditation 32

JEALOUSY LEADS TO TROUBLE

READ DANIEL 6:4-5

Lauren slumped in the principal's office with her head in her hands. She couldn't believe what Amy had just done to her! She had thought the two of them were friends.

Lauren remembered Amy's sly smile as Mrs. Horn took Lauren roughly by the arm and led her to the front office. She recalled her sinking feeling when, in front of the whole class, Amy had accused Lauren of copying her homework and stealing answers out of Amy's desk.

It all started when Mrs. Horn asked Amy to answer a geography question that Lauren answered incorrectly. Amy sat for a moment and looked sheepishly at her teacher. "Uh . . . I . . . I have the same answer as Lauren does, Mrs. Horn," Amy said.

Amy looked at her friend in the next row and asked, "Lauren, how did you get my answers? Did you copy them down at break?" Lauren stuttered and fumbled over her answer. She was so shocked that Amy would accuse her of such a thing that she sat speechless. Amy hadn't been in the hallway at break. *She* must have been the one to steal the answers!

"Miss Overton, you know that I do not tolerate cheating in my classroom," Mrs. Horn said sharply to Lauren, glaring over her black reading glasses. "Let me see your homework sheet. Right this minute, young lady!"

Lauren handed the sheet to Mrs. Horn, and the teacher placed it right next to Amy's. Sure enough, all the filled-in blanks on the photocopied sheet were exactly alike. "That's it!" Mrs. Horn cried. "Let this be a lesson to all you kids. I simply will not tolerate cheaters in my class. Miss

Overton, you come with me. I believe Principal Ruddman will be interested in your story."

So here Lauren sat, waiting for the principal to get off the phone. She felt foolish as Mrs. Ruddman spoke quietly to another school administrator about school finances. Shouldn't she have waited out in the hall or something? But Mrs. Horn had insisted that Lauren sit in this office and wait, and she was in enough trouble already.

"O.K., Jean. Yes, I'll get that memo off to you right away. Uh huh. Uh, Jean, could we perhaps discuss this later? One of my teachers just brought a student in. She's sitting here waiting to talk to me. O.K., thanks. Call you later." Mrs. Ruddman hung up the phone and smiled at Lauren. "Well, Miss Overton. So nice of you to visit me today. My goodness, I don't believe I've ever seen you in here before. Mrs. Horn looked pretty upset there a minute ago. What's up?"

After Lauren had finished her side of the story, Mrs. Ruddman tapped her pencil and thought for a second. Then she said, "Sounds like you've been double-crossed by your classmate, Lauren. I know all about Amy Thompson. Other teachers have discussed her performance with me in the past. Maybe Amy lied to get you in trouble because she was jealous of your good grades. I think Amy's under a lot of pressure, having an older sister who did so well in Mrs. Horn's class two years ago. Don't you worry about it, Lauren. I'll get to the bottom of this."

Lauren breathed a big sigh of relief. She knew she could trust Mrs. Ruddman to find a good solution to the problem. But what about Amy? She'd probably have to stay after school and inside on breaks. *Maybe I'll stay in with her and talk to her about her schoolwork,* Lauren thought to herself. *Yeah, I think I will. Even though Amy hurt me, I still want to be her friend.*

> Lord, sometimes we're falsely accused by people who are jealous of good things we've done, as was Daniel in today's passage. Help us to be able to deal with such problems. Give us grace to react in a way that pleases you.
> Amen.

Meditation 33

SOUND FAMILIAR?

READ DANIEL 6:6-9

Some people believe that history repeats itself. Maybe you believe that too—especially when you look at the clock ten minutes into an hour-long history lesson.

As a history major in college, I studied the rise and fall of various nations and many powerful leaders. And I learned that history taught each of these leaders that their rule wouldn't last forever. The kingdoms of ancient Babylon, Greece, and Rome all came to an end.

In more modern times we've seen formerly great leaders and nations fall too. Take Adolph Hitler in Germany, for example. Or look at the fall of communism and the breakup of the Soviet Union in recent years.

Daniel had the misfortune to see several kingdoms rise and fall in his lifetime. As a young man, remember, he was taken as a captive to Babylon. His own kingdom of Judah and his own king Jehoiakim fell before his eyes as Daniel and his people marched to this foreign land. One kingdom down.

Living and working in Babylon, Daniel saw two different leaders gain power. Nebuchadnezzar turned his rule around and eventually praised God. Belshazzar let his pride get in the way of ruling rightly, and he was killed when Babylon fell. Two kingdoms down.

Now we see the third kingdom and its powerful ruler, Darius. Can you predict what happened to this ruler?

Our passage for today shows history once again repeating itself. The sly satraps, jealous of Daniel's power, have finally found a way to get Daniel in deep trouble and make themselves look good in the king's eyes at the same time. They swagger into the throne room and praise Darius up and down:

"O King Darius, you're the greatest! There's nobody greater than you in the whole earth! And that's not just us talking, Darius. We've taken a vote among all the rulers of your great kingdom! That's right—all the royal administrators, prefects, satraps, advisors, and governors think that you're superhuman in your wisdom and power.

"We want everyone else to think so, too, O king. So why not issue a decree that will make everyone bow down and pray to you for the next thirty days? It'll start your rule out with a bang and set the tone for the rest of your reign. Well, what do you say, O great one?"

The king rubs his chin, and a wide grin spreads over his face. He thinks, *Yeah, why not? After all, I am the ruler of this kingdom. If anybody needs anything, they come and ask one of my governors, who comes and asks me. Why not have all the people pray to me? They'll start to see me as a god, and that can't be all bad.*

Sound familiar? Remember Nebuchadnezzar and the idol he set up and commanded everyone to worship? These two kings both made the mistake of putting something else in place of the God of heaven and earth—the true God of Daniel and the Israelites.

Darius let himself get talked into something that he would later regret. His selfish pride swelled to the size of a watermelon, and his head followed suit.

Just as in Nebuchadnezzar's case, God was watching this little man set himself up as a god. And we can assume God wasn't too happy about it. But instead of intervening, God decided to let Darius learn the error of his ways all by himself. Keep reading and you'll find out how.

> Lord, once again we see a proud man getting carried away with himself and his power. Help us to learn from the result of his actions. And help us to avoid making the same mistake in our own lives.
> Amen.

Meditation 34

THE POWER OF PRAYER

READ DANIEL 6:10

Some guys just don't give up. Daniel, hearing that King Darius has decreed that all people should pray only to him, turned on his heel and headed up to his prayer closet. He'd been praying and worshiping God in this manner for years. No selfish decree from any arrogant king was going to stop him now.

Daniel knew how powerful prayer was. He'd seen the mighty strength of the God of the Israelites. So even though Darius's new law would only be in effect for thirty days, Daniel was not about to betray his trust in God. Knowing the dangers, Daniel "got down on his knees and prayed, giving thanks to his God, just as he had done before."

Prayer is a wonderful gift from God. By praying, you and I and all people have a direct line to our Father in heaven. That means prayer is extremely powerful stuff. Every day, no matter where we are, we can speak with God just as we would a good friend.

Many people pray only when times get tough, like when they're out of money or when they're in trouble: "I really need your help on this test, Lord. I know I haven't studied for it very well . . . O.K., maybe I haven't studied at all. But if I fail this test, I'll have to go to summer school. So please, can you help?"

Other people pray when they want something really badly, as if God is some kind of Santa Claus who will grant our wishes if we're good. But those are the wrong reasons for prayer—they're selfish reasons. We can learn some lessons about prayer from Daniel.

Why did Daniel pray? Was it just to help out of a tough spot? No. Did he want something that he didn't have yet? No. Daniel 6:10 knocks out any possibility of those being the reasons for Daniel's prayers.

Daniel's body language as he prayed revealed his reverence for God: Kneeling showed humility. Facing Jerusalem was a reminder of Daniel's belief that God would bring that city back to its former glory. The fact that he prayed three times a day proved his constant dependance on

God. By staying on his daily prayer schedule, Daniel was continually seeking God's guidance.

How much do you pray? For many Christians, mealtimes provide the most obvious opportunity for prayer. When you sit down to eat, it's natural to thank God for the steaming food on your plate—even if it's lumpy oatmeal.

But God wants you to know that you can approach him at any time of the day, for whatever reason. In fact, God encourages you to stay in constant contact with him, just as Daniel did. Whether you pray

- before deciding how to talk to your non-Christian friend about Christ, or
- when you hear your friend is sick, or
- after you find out that you're starting in Saturday's basketball game, or
- because you want to thank God for keeping you safe on the scariest roller coaster you've ever been on,

God is waiting to hear you. He has the sharpest hearing in the universe; he never gets tired of listening to you talk; and you can trust him completely with whatever is troubling you. Talk to God—right now—in prayer.

I never have to ask if you're listening to me, God. Thank you for that. Help me to think of praying to you often, no matter what situation I find myself in. And thank you, in advance, for your answers.
Amen.

Meditation 35

DARE TO BE A DANIEL

READ DANIEL 6:11-13

This passage tells of Daniel's enemies reporting to King Darius that Daniel has broken the new law. They know that this powerful Hebrew has been bowing in prayer before his God, worshiping and asking for guidance—just as he does every day. They are delighted that their plan has worked, and their jealous hearts are gleeful as they report to Darius.

Risking death by bowing in prayer, Daniel makes a brave stand for his God. He's thumbing his nose at Darius and his advisors, who have tried to make an earthly king into a god. Daniel knows where true power resides, and he courageously stands for what he knows is right.

Many bold individuals in our church's history have followed Daniel's example.

The New Testament book of Acts tells the story of Stephen, a deacon in the early church. He was described as being "full of God's grace and power." He performed many marvelous acts in Jerusalem, all in the name of Jesus.

Because of his witness, the powerful Jews in the city called him to trial. The entire chapter of Acts 7 tells of Stephen's words to the Sanhedrin—the highest religious court of his day. Read it and you'll see how bold Stephen was in the face of the angry court. He wasn't afraid to "tell it like it is" to these powerful men. He took a stand for his Savior, Jesus, and he paid for his convictions with his life.

Hundreds of years later, several men in Europe stood up against angry church leaders for what they knew was right. They spoke, wrote, and preached that the Christian church had begun to accept unbiblical practices. Risking punishment, John Wycliffe, Jan Huss, Martin Luther, John Calvin, and many other brave Christians defended their beliefs. Together they ushered in the Protestant Reformation, from which all churches in the Reformed/Presbyterian tradition stem.

In our own century, a man named Martin Luther King, Jr. stood up for what he knew was right too. He knew that people of different skin colors shouldn't hate each other—especially if they were Christians. He challenged the people in the United States and throughout the world to stop separating from one another because of race. He took his message from his own church pulpit all the way to Washington, D.C.

All of these people, Daniel included, have something in common. They were brave enough to work for what they knew was right, and their words remain with us today. God has allowed us to hear their stories so that we can learn from their example. These stories, and countless others like them, inspire us to live for God and his Son Jesus Christ—no matter where we live or what we do.

When people pressure you to act against what you know is right, don't be afraid to take a stand for Jesus. He calls you to do just that. He wants you to be bold for him, even though you may be mocked or laughed at.

Sounds hard, you say? As I said before, many people have followed Daniel's example. When the time comes, be encouraged by his bravery and his love for God.

God will be pleased with you just as he was with his great hero of faith, Daniel.

> *Father, I thank you for the brave men and women who stand up for you in this world of sin. Every single day, Christian people show your love to millions of people. Help me to be one of those brave Christians, even when the going gets tough.*
> *Amen.*

Meditation 36

THAT LITTLE VOICE INSIDE YOUR HEAD

READ DANIEL 6:14-15, 18

"Just forget about it, Liz," Lizzy whispered to herself as she lay awake in bed. "She had it coming, and you know it. She knew it. Everybody knew it."

Lizzy turned and looked at the clock. It said 12:40 A.M.

"She never should have said that about me in the first place," Lizzy mumbled through clenched teeth. "She knew I would be embarrassed about my new braces."

Lizzy's clock radio hummed quietly. As she listened in the darkness, pictures flashed before her eyes. She remembered the taunting words she had shouted out at the top of her lungs, right there in the hallway. She remembered Julia's face as it turned away from her. She remembered the tears that welled up in Julia's eyes and spilled down her cheeks. Lizzy had laughed at her then, right along with the rest of them. But she remembered that while she was laughing, she felt a little sick to her stomach.

That feeling had lasted all through the day. It got worse when she saw Julia hurry to get her coat and head for the door the minute the bell rang. She could still see Julia limping across the field toward her house, her shorter leg slowing her progress as the large orthopedic shoe that she wore on her left foot got bogged down in the sand.

Why did these images bother Lizzy so much? Why couldn't she get to sleep? Why did she keep picturing Julia crying in her room—that room where Lizzy had spent so much time just last summer?

"Hmmph!" Lizzy groaned as she turned over. "I've got to get to sleep *sometime* tonight. Maybe if I lie on my stomach . . ."

Perhaps you know what kept Lizzy tossing and turning for half the night. It's the same thing that kept Darius awake in the passage that we read today. What kept them awake is that little voice that whispers to each of us. It's called *conscience*, and it usually speaks loudest when we've done something wrong.

What is a conscience? *Webster's Collegiate Dictionary* says that conscience is "the sense or consciousness of the moral goodness or blameworthiness of one's own conduct, intentions, or character together with a feeling of obligation to do right or be good." Big help, right? What that means is that God has given all humans—regardless of whether they love God—an inborn sense of what is right and what is wrong.

Darius learned just how well his conscience worked on the night he sentenced Daniel to the lion's den. The minute his shifty-eyed advisors blew the whistle on Daniel, Darius knew he'd been had. Suddenly the evil intentions of these men were clear as crystal. At the same split second, his own selfish pride and ignorance hit him like a sledgehammer. How could he have done this to Daniel, one of his most trusted advisors? How could he have listened to these untrustworthy men? Blameworthy? You bet. That was Darius.

He knew he had to do something about it. But what? The law he had made was unchangeable. All he could do was sit. And worry. And wait. And sweat. . . .

Lizzy watched the green-blue light on her clock-radio blink to 1:20 A.M. Suddenly an inspiration washed over her in the darkness—it hit her like a flash as Julia's face hovered in front of her eyes for the twentieth time. She knew what she had to do.

She slipped out from under damp covers and found her way to her desk. She flipped the light on and pulled out a piece of paper. "Dear Julia," Lizzy wrote, "I hope you can find it in your heart to forgive me for what I said in the hall. . . ."

> Lord, thank you for giving me that little voice inside my head that tells me when something is right or something is wrong. Help me to listen to that voice and to be honest with myself and with you when I've done something wrong.
> Amen.

Meditation 37

DANIEL'S STORY
(PART 1)

READ DANIEL 6:10-13

"My Lord, once again I come to you for help. I am an old man now, and I pray to you as I have been doing for years. You have always been here for me, and for all these years I have tried my best to serve you and to do what is right in your eyes.

"Now Darius has decreed that all people must put aside their own gods and pray to only him for the next thirty days. You know I cannot do that, my Lord. I cannot deny you and bow my knee to another. No matter what happens, I know that you are stronger than any earthly king, and that you will stand by me."

There. I have done it. For the first time in my career as a ruler over this land, I have deliberately broken a law that my king laid down. I know men who work in the king's court will hold this against me, for they crave power. They know my daily habit of praying to the God of Israel for guidance.

Although I suspect that these same men were behind Darius's decree in the first place, I have no proof. They have been strangely silent around me for the past few days, and that is why I suspect them. In fact, I saw several of them standing on the corner in the marketplace, watching me as I walked home today.

I must be prepared to answer if they ask me what I've been doing. And if they ask, I'll know they've been plotting to have me killed. But I refuse to lie. I refuse to deny my God—the one, true, living God of the Israelites.

Aha! There it is—the fateful knock on the door. I'm sure it's them. I'll bet they've already sent a messenger to the palace to tell the others that their plan is working. Let's just see which ones are brave enough to face me. . . .

"What do you want?"

"Pardon us, Daniel, for disturbing your afternoon routine. We know how important it is—whatever it is that you do in here. By the way . . . just what *were* you doing, anyway?"

"Praying to my God, as is my custom."

"Aren't you aware of the new law Darius decreed that no one is to pray to any of their gods for the next thirty days? Don't you know that your king wants you to bow the knee to him only?"

"I am fully aware of the king's decree."

"Well, then, perhaps you'd better come with us. Guards! You are witnesses to this man's confession. Take this old man—this . . . *criminal*—to the palace. Better yet, take him to the king's prison. I'm sure that's where Darius will want him when he hears what Daniel's done."

It's over. The guards bind me tightly and push me toward the palace. We are certainly causing a commotion in the marketplace—men, women, and children look at me sadly. Others turn away. They must think I've betrayed my king—stolen some money or disobeyed an order.

As far as I'm concerned, I haven't disobeyed. Whatever may happen to me, I know I've obeyed the law of my true King—the God of heaven and earth. I am an old man, and for my entire life I've walked in God's way. My God has always been faithful to me and has blessed the work of my hands.

The prison looms in the distance. I've been there before, but only as an inspector. I never thought I'd walk through those doors as a prisoner! I'm too old to put up a fight, too old to try to escape the strong hands of these young guards. But my life is not in their hands—my life is in much stronger hands. I can count on God's hands to protect me, no matter what.

> Father in heaven,
> Daniel was brave to stand up for you.
> Thank you for giving him the strength to endure,
> to trust in you no matter what.
> Amen.

Meditation 38

DANIEL'S STORY (PART 2)

READ DANIEL 6:12-18

I've waited in this prison for hours now. Nothing seems to be happening with my case . . . perhaps the king has delayed passing sentence on me until tomorrow.

Ah, what a beautiful sunset. It's glowing in through the window of this filthy cell. Perhaps I'll spend the night here after all. . . .

Wait! What's that? It sounds like a crowd of men approaching my cell! Other prisoners are yelling . . . it must be the king's servants. Perhaps they'll bring me to see Darius. Yes! If they bring me to the king, I'll be able to give a reasonable defense for my actions. They're unlocking the door now. . . .

"Daniel! It is my duty to tell you that you displeased King Darius by your actions earlier today. As you have chosen to recklessly break the king's solemn decree, you have been sentenced to death. Darius has ordered that you be thrown into the den of lions—immediately! Darius's decrees may not be broken, Daniel. As a high official in this government, you should have known that. Now you will pay for your crimes against this empire!"

Lions! How could Darius give me such a sentence? How? HOW?

The guards yank me from my cell and back we go into the city streets. Officials light torches to show the way to the den of lions. My knees are so weak I can hardly stand, but the guards hurry me along. Oh my Lord, please rescue me! Please come to my aid!

We've reached the pit now, and there's King Darius! Why didn't he give me a chance to explain? Why didn't he allow me to tell my side of the story? Here he comes now. . . .

"Daniel! Oh, how my heart aches to see you here! I know that you've prayed to your God in violation of my command. And the law of the Medes and the Persians dictates that I must carry out the sentence against you. I have tried all day to find some way to spare you, but the laws of the land cannot be changed. Guards! Lower this old gentleman into the pit. And Daniel, may your God, whom you serve continually, rescue you!"

The pit is dark and dusty, and it reeks of animal droppings and rotten meat. I take one last look at the sunset as it fades in the west.... Now the guards lower me into the hole and seal it with a stone. I cannot possibly escape! The only thing I can do now ... is pray.

"O my Lord, soon the keepers will release the lions into this pit. They'll charge down those ramps and see me here. I know those beasts are starving, Lord. The keepers mistreat them terribly so they'll be ferocious! Still, I know you can save me. My life is in your hands, my Lord."

Here they come! Snarling, hungry, powerful, and vicious, they eye me and lick their chops. What an awful fate! What a horrible way to die! My legs give way and I drop down into the dirt. The largest of them comes my way and ...

What's this? He's sniffing me all over, but not coming in for the kill! Is he just toying with me, torturing me as he would some helpless animal in the wild? The other lions are circling and watching their leader. Will one of them attack if this one doesn't? Their ribs are sticking out—they must be starving. Why don't they make a move toward me?

He ... he's lying down! He's looking away from me and lying down! This ... this must be the work of God! Yes, for without God's protection, I'd surely be in pieces by now. The other lions are picking at some old bones in the corner of the room. One sits down by me and cleans her paws with her tongue. These beasts are ignoring me! It's as if they don't even see me—like I'm not even here!

Praise God, I'm saved! Thank you, God, for answering my prayers once again! Thank you! Thank you!

> *Powerful Father,*
> *I praise you along with Daniel for your protective hand. You watched over Daniel and kept the lions from touching him. Thank you for working this amazing miracle!*
> *Amen.*

Meditation 39

DANIEL'S STORY (PART 3)

READ DANIEL 6:19-28

Well, what a night this has been! I bet that no other man in history has ever spent a night watching lions stalk around him. I think they're starting to get jumpy—two of them just had a brief argument that turned into a noisy, teeth-baring dispute. But not one of these beasts has even looked in my direction for the last few hours.

These poor animals! They're so thin, so dirty. Just think how beautiful these creatures would be in the wild—and how powerful. I'm sure the largest of them was once king among the beasts in the jungle where he was captured. What a wonderful creature he is! Looks like he gets more food than the rest of the pack. They probably don't eat until he's eaten his fill. Of course, none could argue with him, given their condition.

What's this? The keepers have raised the gate and have placed meat on the ramp to draw the lions back to their cages. Look at them scramble! They kick up a cloud of smelly dust. I'll just sit quietly, so the keepers don't hear that I'm still alive.

The guards are removing the rock above me now. Yes, I can see a faint light, as if the sun is just coming up. Looks like I've survived the night! Won't the king's servants be surprised to see me? Their jaws will hit the ground! Wait . . . isn't that Darius's face up there?

"Daniel! Servant of the living God! Has your God, whom you serve continually, rescued from the lions?"

"O king, live forever! My God sent his angel, who shut the mouths of the lions. They have not hurt me, because he found me innocent. Nor have I ever done any wrong before you, O king."

"Guards! Quickly! Take Daniel out of that wretched pit! That's it, look sharp. Have you got him? Good. Now bring him to me.

"Daniel, I can't believe you're still alive! Let me look at you. Are you all right? Did those beasts harm you?"

"No, my king. My God—the God of heaven and earth—has spared me. I trusted in him, and he has once again been faithful to me. So, apart from needing a good hot bath, I'm just as healthy as I was when you left me."

"What wonderful news! When my advisors told me that you broke my decree, I understood their plan. What's worse, they used *me* to get to you! Well, from now on, I will consult you before signing any decree into law. And those who have plotted against you will pay for what they've done. You, Daniel, have been a wise and faithful servant.

"What these other men have done is an act of betrayal that far surpasses breaking any of my written decrees. They have betrayed my trust. Guards! Take those men into custody at once! And since they wanted to see Daniel thrown to the lions so badly, I pronounce the same sentence on them! Carry out my decree immediately, or I'll have you thrown in along with them!"

The guards place me on a platform and carry me to the king's palace. I'll be well cared for after my night in the lion's den.

Well, now Darius knows. He's seen for himself that the God of Israel is the one true God of heaven and earth, just as Nebuchadnezzar and Belshazzar did. This must have been what God intended all along—to show his power and glory to Darius. Praised be the name of the God of heaven and earth!

> Lord, you used Daniel's situation so that kings and rulers would be able to see your strength. I praise you that I know of your power through this story.
> Amen.

Meditation 40

A LOOK BACK

REREAD YOUR FAVORITE STORY FROM DANIEL.

We've come to the end of our look at the life of Daniel. Seen some pretty amazing things, haven't we? What story is your favorite?

Perhaps you've reread the story of Shadrach, Meshach, and Abednego in the fiery furnace from Daniel 3. Maybe you've gone back to Daniel 4 and watched Nebuchadnezzar turn from a pride-filled monarch into a grass-eating monster. Maybe you just *had* to flip to Daniel 5 for one last look at that mysterious hand scratching letters on the wall. Or perhaps you've looked back at Daniel's adventure in the lions' den.

Whatever story you've chosen as your favorite, you need to look carefully for two things: first, God's care and concern for the people who were faithful to him; second, God's power over everything and everyone in this world. No matter what the threats were, Daniel and his friends showed the world exactly where they stood. They weren't about to obey anyone who told them to deny God. Going against God's will never seriously entered their minds.

They had seen God's power early on in a small way, when they chose not to eat from the king's table. When they were later compared to the other young men who were being trained for service in Nebuchadnezzar's court, Daniel and his friends looked better—much better. From that small beginning, they knew they needed to follow God's rule for their lives.

Later on, when their faith in God was tested, they held to that rule. Even when threatened with death, they refused to give in or deny God. And when they faced the heat of the fire or the claws and teeth of the powerful lions, their faith in God strengthened them. With wonder and praise, these men walked out of their death chambers without so much as a scratch. Wouldn't you follow and praise a powerful God who had saved you from those terrible places? They had more proof than they needed of God's awesome might.

I think verses 26 and 27 of Daniel 6 best summarize the themes of this first part of Daniel, don't you? Please take a second to reread this short passage.

The God who saved those faithful men so long ago is the same God we worship today. Our God hasn't changed a bit since the day he pulled Daniel out of the pit. He still watches over his people. He is still more powerful than anyone or anything on earth, and he always will be. He still protects and saves those who turn to him in love.

Since Daniel's time, God has provided a way to save all people from death. Through his only Son, Jesus Christ, he has given every person on earth the opportunity to live forever—if only they'll confess that Jesus is the one way that they can be saved from their sins.

Daniel, his friends, and all the Israelites of the Old Testament were waiting for Jesus. Moses' words in the book of Genesis promised them a Savior would come and save them from their sins. And other Old Testament books gave more information about this Savior. If you want to see an amazing description of Jesus that was written hundreds of years before his birth, check out Isaiah 9:2-7 and Isaiah 53 with your parents.

That's the Savior we worship today. That's the Jesus we honor with our actions when we truly love him and want to serve him. The Messiah the ancient Jews waited for has come, and you and I know him personally. Isn't that terrific?

You may be finishing this book with this last meditation, but don't forget about Daniel and his friends. Perhaps you had already heard about Daniel before you opened this book. If so, I hope these meditations have given you a little different glimpse into who Daniel was and what he and his friends did in service to God.

Remember their example. When times get tough, stand tall in service to God. God won't ever let you down when you tell others that you love him. Dare to be a Daniel!

Thank you, Father, for the assurance that you will always be close to me, watching over whatever I do. Sometimes the world can be a tough place to live. Help me to let others know how wonderful it is to live with the knowledge that the Creator of the universe knows me by name and loves me for who I am.
Amen.